AIR WAR IRAQ

Cover Picture: F-15C Eagle of the 1st Fighter Wing

Back Picture: F-117 Night Hawk

Title page picture: USAF F-16 Fighting Falcons

Right: A Royal Australian Air Force F/A-18 Hornet

Overleaf: The 379th Air Expeditionary Wing at Al Udeid brought together US, British and Australian aircraft to form the largest strike wing in the Middle East.

AIR WAR IRAQ

TIM RIPLEY

Pen & Sword
AVIATION

First published in Great Britain by
Pen and Sword Aviation 2004

British Library Cataloguing-in-Publication Data
A catalogue record for this book
is available from the British Library

ISBN 1 84415 069 0

Printed in Singapore by: Kyodo Printing Co. (Singapore) Pte Ltd.

For a complete list of Pen & Sword titles please contact
Pen & Sword Books Limited
47 Church Street, Barnsley, South Yorkshire, S70 2AS, England
E-mail: sales@pen-and-sword.co.uk
Website: www.pen-and-sword.co.uk

Contents

Notes

1. For ease of recognition the place names used throughout are those in general usage in the international media. Many locations in the Middle East have multiple spellings in Arabic, so confusion often arises.

2. The statistics quoted for missions and sorties used in this report are drawn from the USAF 'By the Numbers' Report, which covers the period 19 March to 19 April 2003.

Dedication
With thanks to ...

US Navy

5th Fleet Public Affairs, Bahrain: Cdr Jeff Alderson, Lt Garret Kasper, Capt Roxi Merritt, Lt-Cdr Steiner and Lt-Cdr Dave Werner, Lt Billy Ray Davis, Lt-Cdr Jeff Carer, USCG

USS *Abraham Lincoln:* Capt Kendall L. Card, CAG Capt 'KC' Albright, Capt Buzby, Lt-Cdr Jeff Bender, Lt Steve Wallburn, Cdr Dale Horan, Master Chief (AVCM) Farrel Briggs, Cdr Rich Simon, Cdr Paul Hass, Cdr George Falok, Lt-Cdr Brad Kidwell, Ensign Bonnie Tanner, JOCS(SA/AW) John Barnett

USAF

Ahmed Al Jaber Airbase: LTC Jennifer Cassidy, USAF PAO; LTC Tom Bergy, 524th Fighter Squadron; LTC 'Skeeter' Gus Kohntopp, 190th FS, Boise, Idaho ANG

Ali Al Salem PAO: Capt John Sheets; Tsgt Neely; LTC Gary Fabricius, 15th Expeditionary Reconnaissance Squadron

Camp Doha ACCC: Maj-Gen Dan Leaf; Maj Dan Snyder, executive officer

USMC Ahmed Al Jaber

Maj T. V. Johnson, 3 MAW PAO; LTC Ed Hebert, 3 MAW staff; Maj Mark Butler, VMA 214; Maj Bruce Laughlin, 3 MAW staff; Maj Jim Wolfe, 3 MAW ground liaison officer

Diplomatic

Mark Ellam, Second Secretary (Political/Press & Public Affairs/British Embassy, Kuwait; Brig Ahmed Al-Rahmani, Director of Morale Guidance & Public Relations for the Kuwaiti Armed Forces; John Morgan, US Embassy, Kuwait. Doha, USAID, James Clad

UK MOD

Simon Wren, Paul Bernard

RAF

DCC (RAF), WCO Ian Tofts
PIC Qatar: Gp Capt Al Lockwood
RAF PIC Kuwait: Spokesman Gp Capt John Fynes, WCO Mike Cairns and Steve Dargan

Ali Al Salem Airbase
Gp Capt Andy Pulford JHF; WCO Paul Lyall, 33 Sqn; WCO David Prowse, 18 Sqn; WCO Dave Robertson, 617 Sqn

Ahmed Al Jaber Airbase: Gp Capt Mike Harwood, Flt Lt John Gunther

British Army

PIC Kuwait: Lt-Col Rob Partridge
PIC Qatar: Maj Will MacKinnley

Royal Marines

PIC Kuwait: Maj Ray Tonner

Royal Navy Bahrain

Cdr Nick Chatwin, Lt-Cdr Steve Tatam, Lt-Cdr Ken Sprowlres RNR, Lt-Cdr 'Mac' Mackenzie, CO of 849 Naval Air Squadron

The Media

The Scotsman, Andrew McLeod, Tim Cornwall, James Hall, Gethin Chamberlain; Daily Telegraph, Michael Smith, Jack Fairweather, Neil Tweedie; Sky News, Tim Marshall, Francis Tusa, Geoff Mead, James Forlong; DPL, Dave Reynolds, Dil Bannerjee; BBC, Andrew Gilligan; BBC Radio 4 Today Programme, Michael Voss; BBC Radio, Paul Adams, Defence Correspondent, Nick Gowing; BBC News 24, Bhasker Solanki; Reuters, Peter Graff, John Chalmers; Air Forces Monthly, Alan Warnes; The Guardian, Richard Norton-Taylor; The Times, Davis Chartes; Financial Times, Roula Khalaf, Emma Jacobs, Gwen Robinson, Victor Mallet; Flight International, Stewart Penny; Tony Holmes; Chris Pocock; Jane's Defence Weekly, Cliff Beale, Ian Kemp, Craig Hoyle, Marion Chiles, Robin Hughes, Peter Felstead; Jane's Intelligence Review, Chris Aaron; News of the World, Keith Gladdis; Press Association, Nick Allen; BFBS, Rosie Laydon; Sunday Express, Tim Shipman; Wall Street Journal, Christopher Cooper. Gary Dimmock

CDISS

Dr Martin Edmonds, Pauline Elliott, Richard Connaughton

LDCAW

Amanda Cahill for her understanding and support during my Middle East 'deployment'.

Introduction

The three-week-long assault on Iraq in March and April 2003 was the culmination of well over a year's worth of preparation. This book looks at how US, British and Australian air commanders pulled together their plans and executed them to overwhelm Iraq's defences.

I spent two months during 2003 in the Middle East, during the build-up and combat phases of Operation Iraqi Freedom, visiting airbases and warships, as well as at US Central Command Headquarters in Qatar.

Even before the first bombs were dropped, it was clear that air power would be the US-led forces' main effort. A visit to Ali Al Salem Airbase a few days before the war made it very obvious that overwhelming force had been massed on Iraq's border. British and American airmen expressed supreme confidence that they would soon overcome Iraq's hapless defences.

The size of the force was massive. Out of some 2,565 aircraft deployed, some 863 were USAF, 372 US Marines and 408 US Navy airframes. In addition, the US Army deployed some 700-plus helicopters. The UK dispatched some 200 aircraft of all types and Australia sent twenty-two.

By comparison, in 1991, the USAF had fielded 830 fixed-wing aircraft, while the US Navy had sent 552 aircraft of all types, the US Marines had dispatched 242 fixed-wing aircraft and 324 helicopters, and the US Army 1,193. In total the Pentagon had committed 1,624 fixed-wing aircraft and 1,537 helicopters to Operation Desert Storm.

Against the 2003 force the Iraqis could muster only some 200 serviceable aircraft. In just three weeks all organized Iraqi resistance was overcome.

Since the occupation of Baghdad in early April, US-led forces have found themselves occupying Iraq. This has also seen extensive use of air power to support the occupying forces.

This book tells the story of the build-up and the war from the perspective of the US, British and Australian airmen. Unfortunately little has emerged to date from Iraq's airmen and air defence troops, so their story can only be told in part. This is not an account of why America, Britain and Australia went to war against Iraq. That story is for others to tell.

Tim Ripley
Lancaster
September 2003

CHAPTER 1

A Decade of Containment

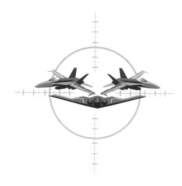

In the heady days after US-led troops drove the Iraqi occupation force from Kuwait in February 1991, the idea that Western forces would still be confronting Saddam Hussein's government for another decade would have seemed ludicrous. The Iraqi president, however, proved more resilient than many imagined, and his armed forces were soon locked in a war of attrition with the American and British aircraft that made daily forays into Iraqi air space to enforce no-fly-zones.

In the wake of the Gulf War cease-fire being signed at Safwan on the Iraq-Kuwait border on 3 March 1991, US President George Bush Snr ordered the rapid return home of the 500,000 American troops who participated in Operation Desert Storm. The USAF 9th Air Force, which provided the air component of US Central Command (CENTCOM), launched Operation Desert Calm between March and August 1991 to redeploy the troops and equipment that had won the war to liberate Kuwait back to their home bases in the USA and Europe.

Iraq had meanwhile imploded, with revolts breaking out in the Shia-populated regions of the south and in the Kurdish areas of the north. Saddam Hussein was able to pull together his battered Republican Guard units from Kuwait and launch counter-attacks. Iraqi Air Force helicopter gunships joined the offensive, but on orders from President Bush USAF McDonnell Douglas F-15C Eagles flying over the combat zones were not allowed to intervene. Public opinion in America and Britain was horrified by television pictures of 350,000 Kurdish refugees fleeing from vengeful Iraqi troops, so President Bush and British Prime Minister John Major were forced to order the launching of Operation Provide Comfort to secure a 'safe haven' for the Kurds in northern Iraq. US European Command deployed a joint task force to Incirlik Airbase in Turkey, first to air-drop relief supplies to the Kurds, and then to mount combat air patrols over the safe haven, above the 36th Parallel, to prevent Iraqi troops returning. By the end of the summer, the refugees had left the mountain-top camps and returned home. Allied ground troops were withdrawn, but the USAF, RAF and French air force kept a wing-sized force of aircraft at Incirlik to protect the Kurds. This arrangement was the origin of the force that has remained in Turkey for over a decade and eventually evolved into Operation Northern Watch.

As part of the United Nations cease-fire resolutions that came into force on 11 April 1991, Iraq agreed to dismantle all its weapons of mass destruction, including long-range missiles, chemical, biological and nuclear weapons. The UN Special Commission to disarm Iraq (UNSCOM) was set up to police the weapons ban. Its inspectors arrived in Iraq during the summer of 1991 and were supported in their work by USAF Lockheed U-2R Dragon Lady reconnaissance aircraft, flying out of Al Taif Airbase in Saudi Arabia. The German government contributed air transport for UNSCOM in the shape of a Luftwaffe C.160D Transall and a pair of

Sikorsky CH-53G Sea Stallion helicopters from Heersflieger Regiment 35. The Transalls shuttled the UNSCOM inspection teams from their headquarters in Bahrain to Iraq, and the big German helicopters were based at Al Rasheed Airport, near Baghdad, to carry teams to inspection sites.

Iraqi efforts to obstruct the inspectors meant that US plans to pull out its forces from the Gulf region had to be put on hold. Combat aircraft, including F-15C Eagles, F-15E Strike Eagles, McDonnell Douglas F-4G Wild Weasels and General Dynamics F-16 Fighting Falcons, were concentrated under the command of the 4404th Wing (Provisional), at Dhahran Airbase, on Saudi Arabia's eastern coast.

To protect the Shia Marsh Arabs from Iraqi air attack, the American, British and French governments decided in August 1992 to establish a 'no-fly' zone over southern Iraq, south of the 32nd parallel. The 9th Air Force's commander, Lt-Gen Michael Nelson, and his staff deployed to Riyadh and took command of Joint Task Force-Southwest Asia (JTF-SWA) for the operation, which was called 'Southern Watch'. The USAF deployed additional aircraft to bring the assets of the 4404WG(P) up to around seventy airframes and personnel to about 4,000. Other support aircraft were based around the region, including McDonnell Douglas KC-10A Extender tankers in the United Arab Emirates and Boeing KC-135 Stratotankers, E-3 AWACS and RC-135 Rivet Joint electronic intelligence-gathering aircraft in Riyadh, Saudi Arabia.

During December 1992 and into January 1993, Iraqi jet fighters launched a series of incursions into the southern and northern no-fly zones. Surface-to-air missiles were also deployed in the zones, threatening British, French and US aircraft. One MiG-25 was shot down by an F-16, in the first successful air-to-air engagement by a USAF Fighting Falcon. Then, on 13 January, a 100-aircraft-strong raid was mounted against Iraqi air-defence sites in the southern zone. Tension continued for almost a week, with daily air strikes against Iraqi SAM sites that had fired on Allied aircraft, and a US Navy BGM-109 Tomahawk cruise missile strike on an alleged nuclear weapon plant near Baghdad. The Iraqis then decided to 'de-escalate' the crisis as a goodwill gesture to the newly inaugurated US President Bill Clinton.

Baghdad was on the receiving end of more cruise missiles in June 1993 after Iraqi agents were arrested in Kuwait, trying to assassinate the former President Bush during a visit. This incident and continued tension over UNSCOM inspections meant the 4404th Wing was still flying daily missions into the southern no-fly zone.

When Iraq began moving ground forces toward Kuwait in October 1994, President Clinton ordered an immediate response. Within days, the new 9th Air Force commander, Lt-Gen John Jumper, and most of his key staff had deployed to Riyadh, where he took command of JTF-SWA. This operation, called 'Vigilant Warrior', also involved the 'plusing-up' of US air assets in the region to more than 170 aircraft and 6,500 personnel. Iraq soon recalled its troops and the crisis passed, but the US decided to retain some 120 aircraft and 5,000 personnel in theatre in case Hussein repeated his bluff. As an additional measure, it was decided to bed-down a squadron of Fairchild A-10A Warthog aircraft in Kuwait itself for the first time.

Concerned about the ability of the US Navy to maintain an aircraft-carrier continuously in the Gulf region, the USAF developed the concept of a squadron-sized Air Expeditionary Force (AEF), which would be able to deploy to the region on two days' notice. The first deployment consisted of eighteen aircraft from the 20th and 347th Fighter Wings, which went to Bahrain's Shaikh Isa Airbase and flew Southern Watch missions. Further deployments of AEFs became routine, with a deployment of thirty F-16s and four KC-135s to Jordan in March/June 1996, and to Qatar in the Gulf later in 1996 and during 1997.

Following a terrorist bombing of the Khobar Towers building complex on Dhahran Airbase in June 1996, the US decided to relocate most of its forces in Saudi Arabia to two remote locations in that country - Eskan Village outside Riyadh, and Prince Sultan Airbase (PSAB) at Al Kharj. The bulk of flying operations relocated to PSAB, while Headquarters JTF-SWA (now renamed Central Command Air Forces (CENTAF) Forward) and US Military Mission personnel moved to Eskan. This operation was code-named 'Desert Focus'. Similar moves to provide additional force protection for US personnel occurred at all other locations where they were based in the Middle East. The British and French also moved the bulk of their forces participating in the no-fly missions to PSAB.

The most serious fighting since 1991 broke out in northern Iraq in August 1996, between rival Kurdish groups, and ending a US-brokered cease-fire. One group appealed to Baghdad for assistance. Saddam Hussein launched his forces into the safe haven, routing anti-Baghdad Kurdish and Iraqi forces. The US responded on 3 September 1996, by launching 'Desert Strike'. Boeing B-52 Stratofortress aircraft of the 2nd Bomb Wing and US Navy ships in the Gulf launched twenty-seven cruise missiles against targets in southern Iraq. President Clinton also ordered the Southern Watch no-fly zone extended to the 33rd Parallel, which meant it now reached to just south of Baghdad. The Iraqi incursion severely undermined links between the anti-Baghdad groups and the US government. Several thousand anti-Baghdad opponents were later flown to America by the US government. The French now decided to pull out of patrolling the northern no-fly zone and refused to patrol beyond the 32nd Parallel in the south.

During late 1997 and into 1998, Iraqi intransigence about UNSCOM inspections continued, along with threats to attack USAF reconnaissance aircraft. The US CENTAF headquarters and support unit personnel and aircraft deployed to the Middle East to augment forces already in the region as preparation began for a major strike against Iraq. After a compromise between the UN and Iraq in March 1998 removed the immediate prospect of military action, US forces totalling about 35,000 personnel remained on heightened alert in the Gulf region. Of these, some 9,000 were USAF personnel.

By the autumn of 1998, the UNSCOM crisis had reached a climax. The inspectors were ordered out by Washington, and military action appeared imminent. A massive air strike was called off in November when a last minute solution looked possible. American and British aircraft went into action on 16 December in the first hours of a four-day bombing effort called 'Desert Fox' against targets involved in the production of weapons of mass destruction or supporting the Republican Guard. Objections by the Saudi and Turkish governments meant that the brunt of the effort was born by carrier-borne aircraft from the USS *Enterprise*, cruise-missile-firing B-52s based on Diego Garcia, British Tornado GR1s and USAF F-117s based in Kuwait, while Rockwell B-1B Lancers operating from Oman made their combat debut. Saudi- and Turkish-based USAF and RAF aircraft were relegated to flying fighter sweeps and suppression of enemy air defence (SEAD) missions throughout the operation. The B-52s fired some ninety AGM-86 Conventional Air-Launched Cruise Missiles (CALCMs), and a total of 650 Allied strike missions were flown against a hundred targets. More than one hundred US Navy Tomahawks were fired.

President Clinton and British Prime Minister Tony Blair may have declared Operation Desert Fox a 'complete success', but Saddam Hussein refused to accept back the UNSCOM inspectors and stepped up his SAM attacks on American and British aircraft patrolling the no-fly zones.

On a daily basis combined British and American 'packages' were sent into the northern and southern no-fly zones to ensure Iraqi compliance. This resulted in deadly cat-and-mouse games between Iraqi SAM crews and Allied airmen. When the Iraqis illuminated the intruders with radar or fired SAMs and anti-aircraft artillery at them, the Allied pilots responded in a variety of ways. ARM-88 High Speed Anti-Radiation Missiles (HARMs) were the instant-response weapons to radar illumination. Surface-to-Air Missile (SAM) batteries, anti-aircraft guns and air-defence headquarters were attacked with either Paveway laser-guided bombs or AGM-130 stand-off missiles.

Washington and London had by now modified their air forces' rules of engagement. American and British jets could now bomb not only Iraqi air-defence batteries actively firing on them, but also supporting radar and command-and-control systems directing any engagements. In an attempt to avoid providing the Iraqis with propaganda from the deaths of civilians, US and British pilots had to go to extreme lengths to ensure their bombs hit only air-defence targets. If they came under attack and could not get a 'clean' target to attack because offending anti-aircraft artillery (AAA, or Triple A) or surface-to-air missile (SAM) batteries were in civilian areas, then the pilots had a 'menu' of response options of approved targets, such as Iraqi Air Defence Command's control bunkers, and radar and communications sites, that could be struck.

In the southern no-fly zone, Iraqi air defences threatened US air force or RAF aircraft on more than 320 occasions between December 1998 and May 2000. The Coalition aircraft responded on seventy-four of those. In total, US and British aircraft dropped 500 bombs on Iraq in 2000, compared to 1,500 in 1999. In February 2001, an increase in Iraqi anti-aircraft activity led to a major strike by twenty-four American and British aircraft against five radar and command posts sites near Baghdad.

Almost every front-line squadron in the active-duty USAF, along with a significant number of Air National Guard or Air Force Reserve units, pulled duty in the Gulf region during the 1990s. More than 200,000 sorties were flown over the southern no-fly zone alone.

By late 2000, as President Clinton was in the process of leaving office, there seemed little prospect of the no-fly zone patrols coming to an end, so the USAF continued to invest in infrastructure to support them. Even the JTF-SWA headquarters was moved to PSAB into a new Combined Air Operations Center (CAOC) that was built by a Saudi construction company owned by the bin Laden family.

USAF F-15E Strike Eagles were based at Ahmed Al Jaber Airbase to provide strategic attack capabilities during the late 1990s, and also flew missions from the Kuwaiti airbase against targets in Afghanistan from October 2001 onwards. (US DoD/JCC(D))

*Chartered Antonov An-124s
were used to move RAF
support equipment to Prince
Sultan Airbase in Saudi Arabia
after the base was activated for
no-fly zone patrols in 1996,
following attacks on US
personnel in Dhahran.*
(US DoD/JCC(D))

The USS Shiloh *joins the
bombardment of southern Iraq
with Tomahawk cruise missiles
as part of Operation Desert
Strike in September 1996.*
(US DoD/JCC(D))

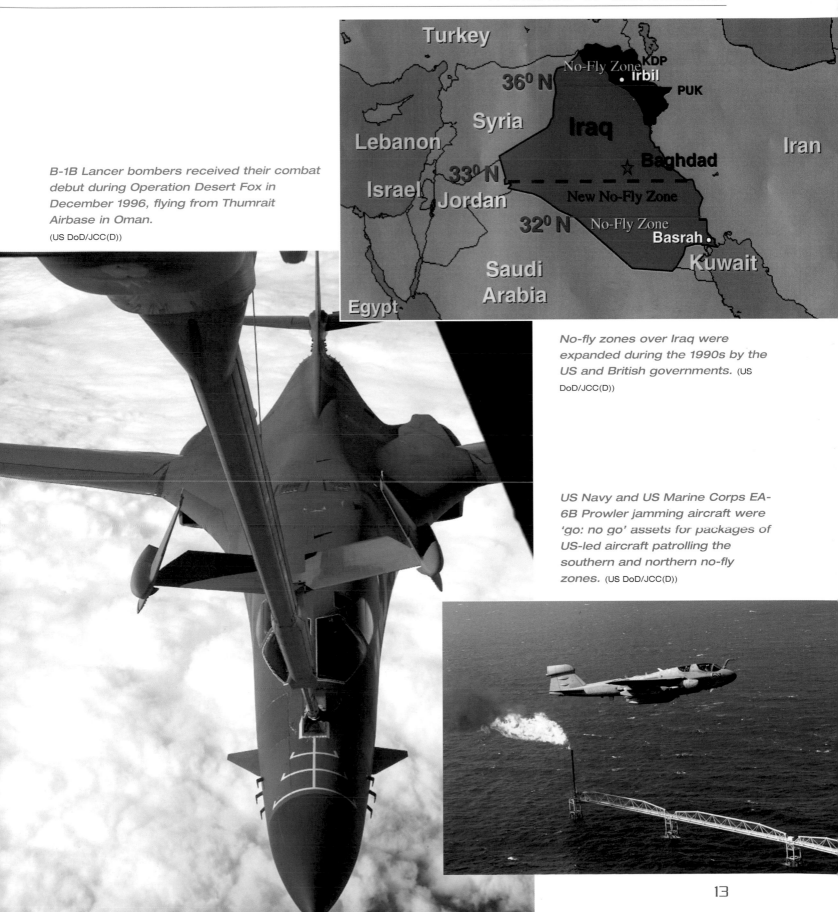

B-1B Lancer bombers received their combat debut during Operation Desert Fox in December 1996, flying from Thumrait Airbase in Oman. (US DoD/JCC(D))

No-fly zones over Iraq were expanded during the 1990s by the US and British governments. (US DoD/JCC(D))

US Navy and US Marine Corps EA-6B Prowler jamming aircraft were 'go: no go' assets for packages of US-led aircraft patrolling the southern and northern no-fly zones. (US DoD/JCC(D))

13

USAF A-10 Warthog ground-attack jets were based at Ahmed Al Jaber Airbase in Kuwait from 1994 onwards, to support US ground troops based in the oil-rich emirate.
(US DoD/JCC(D))

F-117 Night Hawk stealth attack jets based at Ahmed Al Jaber Airbase in Kuwait led strikes into downtown Baghdad during Operation Desert Fox in December 1998.
(US DoD/JCC(D))

Much of the burden of patrolling the no-fly zones fell on the F-15C Eagle air supremacy squadrons.
(US DoD/JCC(D))

AL SAHRA AIRFIELD, IRAQ

Al Sahra Airfield was heavily attacked during Operation Desert Fox in December 1998 because it was suspected of housing unmanned aerial vehicles.
(US DoD)

AL KUT BARRACKS WEST-NORTHWEST, IRAQ

Barracks of the Elite Republican Guard in Al Kut were high on the target list during Operation Desert Fox in December 1998.

(US DoD)

B-52 Stratofortress bombers supported Operation Desert Fox in December 1998 from the British Indian Ocean island of Diego Garcia.
(US DoD/JCC(D))

A-10A Warthog ground-attack jets based at Incirlik Airbase in Turkey mounted intense patrols over Kurdish regions of northern Iraq in April 1991 to deter Iraqi attacks on refugees gathered along the Turkish border. (Tim Ripley)

Iraq's intelligence headquarters in Baghdad was targeted by US Navy cruise missiles after the agency was implicated in a plot to kill former US President George Bush Snr during a visit to Kuwait in June 1993. (US DoD/JCC(D))

HITS IN COMPLEX	🔥
MISSES IN COMPLEX	○
COLLATERAL DAMAGE	△

Iraq's mountainous north was patrolled constantly from April 1991 to March 2003 by US-led aircraft, such as this F-16C Fighting Falcon, operating from Incirlik Airbase in Turkey. (Tim Ripley)

Kuwait's air force was re-equipped during the 1990s with F/A-18C Hornets to replace the aircraft lost during the Iraqi occupation between August 1990 and February 1991.

(McDonnell Douglas)

German Heersflieger CH-53G Sea Stallion heavy-lift helicopters served with the United Nations Special Commission during the 1990s, transporting arms inspection teams around Iraq.

Above: (UNSCOM)
Left: (Tim Ripley)

Arms inspectors from the UN Special Commission scoured Iraq from 1991 to 1998 looking for weapons of mass destruction, such as this chemical rocket. (UNSCOM)

US Navy CH-53E Sea Stallion helicopters were the first aircraft to deliver aid to Kurdish refugees trapped along the border of Turkey in April 1991. (US Navy)

CHAPTER 2

Iraqi Air Defences and Air Forces

From December 2002 to early 2003, on most evenings the peace of the Iraqi capital was shattered by sporadic cannon fire from anti-aircraft batteries positioned on the roofs of high-rise buildings throughout central Baghdad.

This nightly ritual was portrayed by Saddam Hussein's propaganda machine as vigilant actions by his Air Defence Command to defend Iraq from 'aggression' by American and British aircraft. Visitors to the beleaguered city, however, were far from impressed by the military bearing of these scruffy and obviously poorly trained gunners. They seemed just to be firing into the air for the sake of it. There were usually no US or UK jets overhead. The gunner's random pot-shots appeared to be either haphazard firing practice - a dangerous proposition when a heavily populated city lies downrange - or a crude attempt to maintain 'war fever' among the Iraqi people.

To the north and south of the Iraqi capital, more deadly duels took place on an almost daily basis between Iraq's air-defence forces and intruding Western jets attempting to enforce no-fly zones. The US military cited more than 110 separate incidents of Iraqi surface-to-air missile and anti-aircraft artillery fire directed against Coalition aircraft from January 2002 to early August 2002 alone. In mid-May 2002 Iraqi attacks against US and UK jets began to escalate considerably, prompting an increase in retaliatory bombing.

Iraqi air-defence crews in the no-fly zones clearly knew that every time they opened fire they risked being on the receiving end of precision-guided munitions dropped from British or American bombers. Yet on at least 1,100 occasions, or on average thirty-six times a month, since December 1998 they chose to open fire. By late 2002 the Iraqi government claimed US and British bombing had killed 1,477 people and injured 1,358 since London and Washington had imposed the no-fly zones. The vast majority of these casualties were probably not civilians but personnel of the Air Defence Command who were caught in American and British air strikes on their command posts and missile and gun batteries.

Clearly the officers and men of the Iraqi Air Defence Command deployed in the no-fly zones had more mettle that their counterparts based in the relative safety of Baghdad, where US and British bombers rarely ventured. After the élite Republican Guard Forces Command, the air-defence men were considered the regime's most favoured military force. Saddam considered them his best chance to down a US or UK aircraft and capture its pilot, giving him a major propaganda coup over his enemies. If US and British aircraft could be driven from the no-fly zones, even for a few days, it would have given the Iraqi president the room for manoeuvre necessary to launch a deadly strike on rebel groups who had gathered under the limited protection of foreign air power.

The first sign that Saddam Hussein was giving his Air Defence Command preferential treatment was when he removed it from control of the Iraqi Air Force (IQAF) immediately after the Gulf War. This was a reward for the shooting down of some thirty-six Coalition aircraft, and it compared highly favourably with the lacklustre performance of the Air Force, which only managed to shoot down one US fighter - a US Navy McDonnell Douglas F/A-18C Hornet - in air-to-air combat.

Iraqi Air Defence Command personnel were lavished with high salaries, houses and other perks. The organization also had a high priority, just after Saddam's weapons-of-mass-destruction factories, for funding to import foreign equipment in violation of United Nations sanctions. Local arms factories were giving the demands of the command a very high priority. Saddam, moreover, had provided his men with more personnel incentives, offering a cash reward of $5,000 to the air-defence unit that shot down a US or British aircraft, and a $2,500 bonus to the individual who captured a downed flier.

Iraqi exile sources said the Air Defence Command had some 17,000 men under its control in early 2003, based throughout the country. The Iraqis relied on a mix of SAM and AAA systems bought largely during the 1970s and 1980s from the then Soviet Union and France. Some Western systems were captured from Kuwait in 1990 and others were smuggled into the country after the 1991 Gulf War, in violation of the UN arms embargo.

The mainstay of the Iraqi SAM force was some twenty to thirty batteries of Soviet V-75 Dvina (NATO code-name SA-2 'Guideline'), twenty-five to fifty batteries of S-125 Neva (SA-3 'Goa') and thirty-six to fifty-five batteries of 9M9 Kub (SA-6 'Gainful') radar-guided SAMs. The exact number of launchers operational in early 2003 was unclear, but it was probably in the region of a hundred or so of each type of system. The Iraqis established local repair facilities for all these systems and limited production facilities to manufacture replacement missiles. In 1983 the Iraqis bought Roland SAM launchers and 300 missiles from France, and some of these were still operational in early 2003. All these weapon systems were dependent on radar surveillance and guidance, and the Iraqis possessed an abundance of radars organic to them. For area surveillance, the Iraqis had a number of radars, including Soviet P-14 'Tall Kings' and French-made Thomson-CSF Volex IIIs.

To fill out its defences, the Iraqis possessed some 4,000 AAA guns, ranging from 12.7 mm up to 23 mm, 37 mm and 57 mm calibre weapons. Thousands of short-range radar and heat-seeking guided SAMs, including Strela-2 (SA-7 'Grail'), Romb (SA-8 'Gecko'), Strela-1 (SA-9 'Gaskin') and Igla-1 (SA-16 'Gimlet') were also in Iraqis hands and were used to provide local protection of the bigger radar-guided SAMs or army units.

The nerve centre of the Air Defence Command was a large underground bunker complex at the Al Muthanna airfield in central Baghdad. It had an operations centre that controlled all its subordinate units in real-time, thanks to a fibre-optic communications network built in the 1980s. In 2001 the US government accused the Chinese of sending technicians to upgrade this network. From the operations centre, radar surveillance, fighter mission control, SAM and AAA batteries were all co-ordinated.

Iraq was split up into four air-defence zones, each with its own sector operating centre (SOC) to control specific engagements. The 1st SOC at the Al Taji complex outside Baghdad controlled the defence of the airspace in the centre of the country. It had command of the bulk of the SAM assets providing protection of the capital and other sensitive locations, such as Saddam's palaces and weapons-of-mass-destruction factories. Its order of battle included at least two missile brigades with 16 SA-2 and SA-3 batteries, as well as scores of independent SA-6 and Roland batteries.

Western Iraq was controlled by the 2nd SOC at Al-Waleed (H-3) Airbase, with some ten SAM batteries at its disposal. The job of challenging US and British aircraft in the southern no-fly zone was left to the 3rd SOC near Tallil Airbase, north west of Basra. It had at least one SAM brigade and scores of AAA batteries.

The 4th SOC at Al-Hurriya Airbase, outside Kirkuk, was tasked with engaging Western aircraft over the northern no-fly zone. It had at least half a dozen SA-2 and SA-6 batteries.

Supporting the SOCs were dozens of radar and electronic warfare detachments. Missile crews and radar operators were trained at the Air Defence Institute at Al Taji.

The Air Defence Command's tactics and operating procedures were based on Soviet lines, with highly centralized command posts controlling every engagement. After 1991 the Iraqis developed their own tactics to counter the US- and UK-imposed no-fly zones. Under Soviet doctrine, land-based weapon systems were closely integrated with fighter aircraft. This tactic had clearly failed in the Gulf War, where Iraqi fighters were outclassed by Western aircraft and were only able to successfully engage Coalition aircraft on one occasion. Heavy jamming of the Iraqi radio communications net prevented co-ordination of air- and ground-based weapon systems. The occasions since 1991 when the Iraqis tried to put up their fighters also ended in failure.

This forced the Iraqis to rely almost entirely on their ground-based systems to take on the British and Americans. They developed great skill at concealing their small number of missile launcher units, until the point at which they decided to fire. Either because they were unable to immediately pin-point the offending launcher or because of fears of hitting civilian-populated areas, American and British crews more often than not were forced to strike against more easily identified radar sites or command posts.

The Iraqis developed great skill at hiding and moving their missile launchers into towns and villages and then bringing them out for 'snap' shots at targets, such as the Lockheed U-2 Dragon Lady and Grumman E-2C Hawkeye engaged in 2001. Those missiles missed, but the crews of the aircraft under attack received a nasty surprise.

The Iraqi fibre-optic cable network gave them a small tactical advantage. They could detect and track targets with their area surveillance radars based outside the no-fly zones and rapidly pass the information to forward-based SAM batteries. This meant they did not have to use their organic radar systems until the very last minute before missile launch, giving them a degree of surprise. The US then deployed a squadron of General Atomic RQ-1 Predator unmanned aerial vehicles to Kuwait to fly surveillance missions in high-risk areas of Iraq. Three were lost to Iraqi fire during the second half of 2001 and another was shot down by a MiG-25 in December 2002.

Saddam devoted considerable amounts of money to boosting the capabilities of his Air Defence Command. New equipment in 2001 and 2002 included mobile SA-3 launcher vehicles that saw action in southern Iraq. Extra fuel cells were installed on SA-2 missiles to allow them to engage high-flying U-2s.

IRAQ'S AIR FORCE

The 1990s were a lean period for the Iraqi Air Force (IQAF). UN sanctions cut it off from sources of replacement aircraft and new technology. US- and British-imposed no-fly zones meant it was reduced to flying in a small area in the centre of the country. It lost a MiG-25 and MiG-29 to US fighters in late 1992 and early 1993 and afterwards did not even dare to engage Western fighters. This, on top of its failure to stop US air raids during the Gulf War, seriously undermined the IQAF's reputation in the eyes of Iraq's president. Particularly damaging to the IQAF's usefulness to Saddam Hussein was the loss of almost all of the prized Su-24 deep strike fleet, which the Iranians refused to return after they fled there during the 1991 Gulf war.

Although there were rumours of the IQAF importing black market spares from Eastern Europe in a bid to boost its lamentable serviceability rates, this was not reflected in any upsurge in air activity, with reports in early 2003 suggesting that it had fewer than 100 serviceable airframes.

Air activity was concentrated at eight main operating bases around Baghdad, Mosul and Kirkuk, as well as a handful of dispersal bases. These bases had largely been renovated, but the IQAF simply did not have the resources to completely rebuild all the hardened shelters and runways destroyed by US and British bombing during Operation Desert Storm.

Bolstered by its key role in crushing the 1991 rebellions, the IAAC enjoyed a more prosperous decade, particularly officers and units with links to the Republican Guard Forces Command (RGFC). A number of special squadrons were formed to support the RGFC in both the IAAC and IQAF.

Table 1. Iraqi Air Force Equipment, Summer 2002	
Personnel	30-35,000
Airframes in inventory	300+
Operational Combat Aircraft	69-93
inc. **Mirage F.1** (multi-role fighter)	13
Mikoyan MiG-21 (fighter-bomber)	15-25
MiG-23 (multi-role fighter)	15-20
MiG-25 (long-range interceptor)	4
Sukhoi Su-25 (close air support)	5-10
Su-22 (ground attack)	15-18
MiG-29 (long-range interceptor)	1
Su-24 (long-range bomber)	1
Il-76 (transport)	1
Al Yammah-A (recce drone)	?
Marakub (based on Mirach 100 target drone)	?
Sarab-B (version of Banshee target drone)	?
L-29 drone (based on Czech jet trainer)	?

Table 2. Operating Bases, Summer 2002

Al-Rashid
Republican Guard Sqn (PA-34 and An-2), Special Transport Sqn (Bell 214ST)

Al Habbaniyah/Al Taqaddum
MiG-29 (6 Sqn), MiG-21 (14 Sqn), MiG-23 (73 Sqn), Su-25 (109 Sqn), Su-22 (44 Sqn)

Al Bakr (Tikrit)
MiG-23 (49?, 63? and 93 Sqns), Su-24 (8 Sqn), Su-22 (5 Sqn), An-24 and An-26 (3 Sqn), Il-76 and PA-34 (33 Sqn)

Al Qadisiya (Al Asad)
MiG-21 (combat training wing)
MiG-21 (17, 47 and 57 Sqns) and MiG-25 (96 Sqn)

Al-Hurriya (Kirkuk)
Su-22 (69 Sqn)

Al Quayara (Mosul)
Mirage F.1 (79? and 89? Sqns) and MiG-21 (9 Sqn)

Abu Gharid, Baghdad
Air Force Academy, three squadrons of EMB-312 and L-39

Dhuloya, Baghdad
Unmanned aerial vehicles

Table 3. Iraqi Army Air Corps Equipment, Summer 2002

Total 500 helicopters, including 120 armed helicopters
(estimated 250+ operational)

Mil Mi-8/17s 'Hip' (transport)

Mi-25s 'Hind' (gunship)

MBB Bo-105s (liaison/attack)

Bell 212STs (transport)

Aérospatiale SA-342 Gazelles (liaison/armed)

SA-316 Alouettes (liaison/armed)

Hughes 500s (liaison/attack)

Pilatus PC-7 and PC-9 fixed wing turbo-props (armed training aircraft)

Table 4. IAAC Main Bases, Summer 2002

Al-Jadida, Baghdad
> HQ Military Aviation

Kirkuk, 1st Wing
> PC-9 (83 Sqn), Mi-17 (4 Sqn), Mi-8 (2 Sqn), SA-316 (30 Sqn), Hughes 500D and SA-342 (84 Sqn)

Taji, Baghdad, 2nd Wing
> Mi-25 (66 Sqn), Mi-17 (55 Sqn), Bo-105 (106 Sqn), SA-342 (22 Sqn)

Kut, 3rd/4th Wing
> SA-342 (88 Sqn), Mi-17 (15 and 99 Sqns)

Al-Swenta, 5th Wing
> PC-7 (107 Sqn), Mi-6, Mk-117, SA-342, Mi-8/17, Bell 214ST (Special Sqn)

Iskandceria, Baghdad, 7th/9th Wing
> (2 Sqn?, 8 Independent Sqn, 77 Special-Purpose Sqn)

Al-Suwaira, Military Aviation School
> Bell 214ST, Hughes 500D/F

Radar Coverage of Southern No-Fly Zone

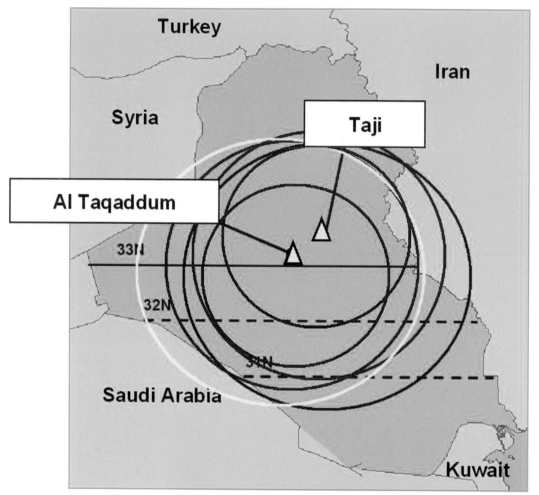

This graphic, showing Iraqi radar coverage, was used in a Pentagon briefing on February 2001 raids on Iraqi Air Defence Command bases.
(US DoD)

This photograph of Tall King area surveillance radar, was used in a Pentagon briefing on February 2001 raids on Iraqi Air Defence Command bases.
(US DoD)

This photograph of Thompson-CSF Volex area surveillance radar was used in a Pentagon briefing on February 2001 raids on Iraqi Air Defence Command bases.
(US DoD)

The Iraqi Air Defence Command's network of bases and command posts is pictured here.
(US DoD)

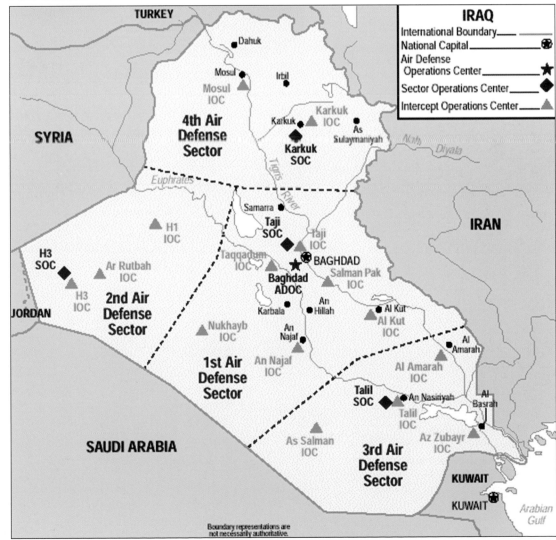

Iraqi Army Air Corps Bell 212s were used for VIP transport and supported Republican Guard units. (US DOD)

Mil Mi-8s (Hip) were the workhorses of the Iraqi Army Air Corps in both transport and attack roles. (US DOD)

This Iraqi MiG-23 (Flogger), pictured at the Yugoslav air force museum next to Belgrade Airport in November 2000, was stranded in Yugoslavia in August 1990 by UN sanctions while it was undergoing overhaul.
(Tim Ripley)

Iraqi Army Air Corps Mil Mi-24 (Hind) attack helicopters spearheaded attacks on Kurdish and Shia rebels in the aftermath of the 1991 war.
(US DOD)

An Iraqi S-60 anti-aircraft artillery battery in firing positions was located by an RAF Tornado through a TIALD system during a patrol over the southern no-fly zone in early 2002.
(BAe Systems)

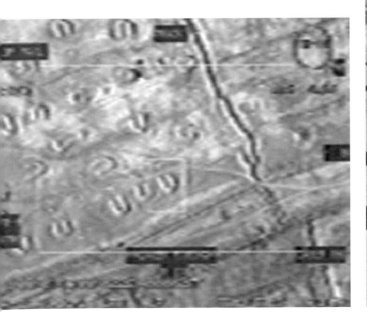

Iraqi 9M9 Kub (SA-6 Gainful) missile crews in Mosul rail yard scan the sky after being overflown by an RAF Jaguar patrolling the northern no-fly zone.

(Vinten Ltd)

Iraq's new mobile S-125 Neva (SA-3 Goa) SAM launcher vehicle in firing position was located by a Predator unmanned aerial drone during a patrol over the southern no-fly zone in late 2001.

(US DOD)

Tallil Airbase was the target of a devastating Coalition air attack during the 1991 Gulf War.

(US DOD)

This Iraqi S-60 57 mm anti- aircraft gun was abandoned in Kuwait in 1991.
(US DOD)

French-made Roland surface-to-air missile batteries were still operational in 2003.
(Tim Ripley)

31

Soviet-supplied and Iraqi-produced versions of the V-75 Dvina (SA-2 Guideline) surface-to-air missiles were the mainstay of Iraq's Air Defence Command.
(US DOD)

Soviet-supplied and Iraqi-produced versions of the S-125 Neva (SA-3 Goa) surface-to-air missile.
(US DOD)

An Iraqi Su-22
(Fitter) is seen
in a hardened
aircraft shelter
at Tallil Airbase
in southern Iraq
in the aftermath
of the 1991 war.
(US DOD)

ZSU-23-4 self-propelled anti-aircraft systems provided low-level air defence for Iraqi Republican Guard units.

(US DOD)

CHAPTER 3

Build-up for War

In the wake of the 1991 Gulf War, US Central Command (CENTCOM) developed contingency plans to attack and defeat Iraq. They were revised annually during the years of the Clinton Administration, but this was a routine exercise as there was little appetite in the White House between 1992 and 2000 for a major war in the Middle East.

This changed with the arrival of the Bush Administration in January 2001 and the installation of Donald Rumsfeld as Defense Secretary and Paul Wolfowitz as his deputy. In the aftermath of the 11 September 2001 attacks on New York and Washington, the political climate in the US changed fundamentally and an attack on Iraq climbed up the agenda, even if it would have to wait until the situation in Afghanistan stabilized during the spring and summer of 2002 for planning to go forward.

Examination of detailed contingency planning for an attack of Iraq now began in earnest. Debates raged within the administration throughout the summer of 2002 over the wisdom of attacking Iraq and how it would be done. The decision to go ahead with an attack on Iraq was made in September 2002. It was decided to try one last round of UN inspections at the behest of the British Prime Minister, Tony Blair. Crucially US President George Bush secured political top cover for his Iraq strategy when both houses of the US Congress passed War Powers Resolutions in October.

The military planning process began in parallel with the political one, with President Bush requesting the Joint Chiefs of Staff to begin preparing contingency plans. They in turn tasked Gen Tommy Franks, the commander of CENTCOM, which had responsibility for all American military operations in the Middle East, to begin detailed planning.

Throughout the late summer and into the autumn of 2002, arguments raged between Franks, Rumsfeld and the White House over the Iraq invasion plan. In the end a compromise was agreed that was soon dubbed the 'rolling start'. This envisaged starting the attack with a 'medium-sized' force of three corps-sized ground formations, backed by massive airpower, but a further 100,000 troops would be held back in reserve until the war started and it became clear if they were needed. Their equipment would be loaded on ships heading to the region, but the troops themselves would remain at their home bases waiting to fly out to the Middle East.

Fundamental to the US war planning was the assessment that the Iraqis would 'fold' early because of poor morale and opposition to the government of Saddam Hussein among large segments of the population. Iraq's government was defined as 'brittle' and likely to crack open as soon as a strong force of US troops arrived in Baghdad.

President Bush's political directive set several operational objectives for Franks's planners to achieve during any military campaign, including:

1. Ending the regime of Saddam Hussein
2. Identifying, isolating and eliminating Iraq's weapons of mass destruction
3. Searching for, capturing and driving out terrorists from Iraq
4. Collecting intelligence related to terrorist networks
5. Collecting intelligence related to the global network of illicit weapons of mass destruction
6. Delivering humanitarian support to the displaced and needy Iraqi citizens

7. Securing Iraq's oil fields and resources

8. Creating conditions for a transition to a representative self-government in Iraq.

The planning process then entered a new phase as Franks allocated tasks to his main air, land, sea and special-operations forces component commanders. During the last three months of 2002, these officers and their staffs examined the details of what was required of them and began what was known as the 'force generation' process. These assessments were sharpened during a series of command post exercises held in the Gulf region during November and December 2002, under the banner of 'Exercise Internal Look'. This, in turn, honed the exact requirements for troops and equipment needed for any war, as well as the diplomatic clearances for basing and over-flight rights in countries neighbouring Iraq. Long-term logistic support measures, including the moving of some pre-positioned equipment from stores in Qatar and Diego Garcia, had already begun. The main bulk of the troops began moving early in January, and the deployment rolled out over the next two months.

Franks also began reorganizing his headquarters staff to allow CENTCOM to fight Iraq while still conducting anti-terrorist operations in Afghanistan and the Horn of Africa. Regional headquarters in Afghanistan and Dijbouti were beefed up to take the pressure off the main CENTCOM staff. An alternative combined air operations centre (CAOC) was activated at the massive Al Udeid Airbase in Qatar to conduct Afghan and Horn of Africa air operations. The main CENTCOM staff was also split, with a 'forward' headquarters being established at Camp As Saliyah under Franks's deputy, Lt-Gen John Abizaid, specifically to run any Iraq operation.

One requirement identified early in the planning process was the need to prevent any pre-emptive Iraqi strikes to disrupt the deployment of US troops in Kuwait. The USA had long based ground troops in Kuwait, and they had been reinforced late in 2001 when US carrier airpower was diverted from the Middle East to support the Afghan campaign.

At the heart of the US battle plan was the need to bring the main bulk of the Republican Guard Forces Command into battle and destroy them. These supposed élite troops were seen as one of the Iraqi government's main 'centres of gravity', and their destruction was seen as a way to engender a 'psychological fracture' in the ruling circle. Once they were gone, the rapid advance of US troops into the heart of Baghdad would be possible, to allow the coup de grâce to be delivered to Saddam Hussein. The assessment was that once the government was seen to be defeated, the population and the mass of the Regular Army would lose heart and give up the fight. To do this job, Franks requested the US Army's V Corps and the I Marine Expeditionary Force (I MEF), with some 150,000 combat troops. The only realistic basing option was in Kuwait because of its friendly government and extensive port facilities. The southern desert was also largely undefended, so US planners believed their main land force would have a relatively free run to the Baghdad region where the Republican Guards Force Command was based, or US airpower would destroy it if it moved south to join battle with the invaders.

In the early US planning it became clear that a corps-sized land force was needed to strike into northern Iraq from Turkey to pin the three Iraqi corps holding the front lines opposite the Kurdish safe haven, preventing them swinging south to held defend Baghdad. The force would then move to secure Tikrit, Saddam Hussein's home town.

While Franks was very successful in winning basing rights from Jordan, Saudi Arabia and the Gulf states for his forces, the 'northern front' ran into trouble during January and February, culminating in the Ankara parliament rejecting the US request to move 60,000 ground troops across Turkish territory. To try to maintain the threat of a northern front, Franks kept the ships carrying the equipment for the 4th Infantry Division in the Mediterranean until the war had started.

The other main pillar of the US plan was a strategic air campaign, backed by special-operations forces, aimed at neutralizing and possibly killing senior members of the Iraqi government. Unlike in 1991, when the strategic air campaign had focused heavily on infrastructure targets, such as bridges, oil refineries and power stations, this time only presidential palaces, government ministries, command bunkers, air-defence sites and locations associated with the weapons of mass destruction programme were to be attacked.

Fundamental to the planning was the need for concentric air, land and sea-borne attacks from north, south and west to rapidly overwhelm Iraq's defences. The aim was not to physically destroy Iraq's armed forces but to neutralize them in order to open the way for US-led forces to attack and kill leading members of the government. In military jargon, this was to be an 'effects'-based campaign.

Special emphasis was placed on giving the US-led air forces the capability to attack high-value targets, such as Saddam Hussein and his immediate circle, on the basis of fleeting intelligence. A cell to manage attacks against so-called 'time-sensitive targets' was set up inside the US air headquarters in Saudi Arabia.

The nerve centre of US air operations in the Middle East was the Combined Air Operations Centre (CAOC) at Prince Sultan Airbase (PSAB), where General Franks's air commander, USAF Lt-Gen Michael 'Buzz' Moseley had his headquarters. The CAOC was classed as a 'weapon system' in its own right, and its computerized communications links allowed the rapid collection of intelligence on targets in Iraq and the dissemination of attack orders to strike aircraft.

Prior to the war, the CAOC had a staff of 672 US, British and Australian staff officers attached, but as conflict neared the number of personnel rose to 1,966. The core of their work was the production of a daily air tasking order, which included all the targeting, routes and communications detail needed for every aircraft and cruise missile sent into Iraqi air space. This centralized system allowed airpower to be concentrated at specific targets and ensured that hundreds of friendly aircraft did not endanger each other.

The CAOC was a true joint service effort, controlling, for example, all the US Navy and British Royal Navy BGM-109 Tomahawk Land Attack Missiles (TLAMs) launched from ships and submarines against Iraqi targets, and all the US Army's Patriot missile defence units in the Middle East.

While the planning for the air offensive against Iraq gathered momentum during 2002, it was not until January 2003 that the flow of additional aircraft to execute the attack began in earnest. This was eased by more than a decade of no-fly zone operations, which meant that most of the communications and logistic infrastructure needed to support the extra aircraft and personnel were already in place at bases around the Middle East.

By the time the war got under way on 19 March 2003, some 466,985 US personnel were in the Middle East, with 233,342 coming from the US Army, 74,405 from the US Marine Corps, 61,296 from the US Navy and the US Air Force providing 54,995, of whom 2,084 came from Air Force Reserve and 7,207 from the Air National Guard. Britain was the largest provider of non-US forces, with 40,905 personnel in the Middle East, alongside 2,050 Australians.

Out of some 1,801 aircraft deployed, some 1,477 were fixed-wing and 186 were helicopters. The largest number were provided by the USAF, which dispatched some 863 aircraft to bases in the Middle East and

Europe for the operation, including 293 fighters, 51 bombers, 22 command and control, 182 tankers, 60 intelligence, surveillance and reconnaissance, 73 special operations and 58 rescue, 111 airlift and 13 other aircraft. The Air National Guard provided 236, and Air Force Reserve 70, of these aircraft. The US Navy managed to muster some 232 fighters, 20 command and control, 52 tanker, 29 intelligence, surveillance and reconnaissance, five airlift and 70 other types of aircraft. The US Marine Corps dispatched some 130 fighters, 22 tankers and 220 other aircraft, mostly helicopters. The British armed forces provided some 200 aircraft and helicopters, and the Australians sent 22 airframes. The US Army deployed some 700 attack, scout and transport helicopters.

Many of these aircraft headed for airbases already in use for Operation Southern Watch missions over the southern no-fly zone or supporting Operation Enduring Freedom in Afghanistan. Other bases had to be activated from pre-positioning equipment and stores maintained at them. Many of the host governments were very sensitive to their public opinion, which was almost universally opposed to any war against Iraq, and deployments had to take place under conditions of great secrecy. Saudi Arabia, Bahrain and the United Arab Emirates banned offensive strike aircraft from operating on their territory and banned media access to their airbases. Qatar, Oman and Jordan all allowed offensive aircraft, but imposed draconian secrecy on US and British deployments to their airbases. The exception to this was Kuwait, which embraced the US war plans with enthusiasm and allowed the US and British use of all their main airbases. When these became full of aircraft and helicopters, field airstrips and helicopter landing pads were constructed in the northern deserts close to the Iraqi border.

As soon as fighter and strike squadrons arrived at bases in the Middle East, planners in the CAOC began to use them for Operation Southern Watch to give the crews experience of countering Iraqi air defences and the procedures for flying in Iraqi air space.

General Moseley had also been making efforts to 'prepare the battlefield' for several months, so that when his forces were sent into action to support the land invasions they would already have destroyed key elements of the Iraqi air defence systems. This effort was dubbed 'Southern Focus' and concentrated on destroying key surface-to-air missile batteries and fibre-optic communications nodes. This took advantage of a change in the rules of engagement that allowed Iraqi command posts and communications sites to be attacked in response to firings on US and

British jets patrolling the no-fly zones. These static targets also had the advantage of being far easier to locate than mobile missile launchers or gun batteries. From June 2002 to early 2003 some 21,736 sorties were flown and 345 targets attacked as part of this effort, which effectively put out of action the air defences in the south and west of Iraq by mid-March 2003.

As the UN political process failed to produce results to the liking of the Bush administration during February, it became more determined to go ahead with the attack, come what may. Rumsfeld and his senior CENTCOM military commanders began pressing for efforts to 'prepare the battlefield' to be stepped up. They wanted to give their air power freedom to attack Iraqi surface-to-surface missile launchers and artillery batteries in southern Iraq. The senior British officers in the Middle East now played their 'red card' and objected. They claimed that this had no legality and had not been approved by the British government. The issue bounced up to the senior levels in both governments. Blair, who was still trying to win approval for a second UN resolution to placate increasing anti-war feeling in his party and cabinet, backed his military men. Rumsfeld was told his pilots could only attack Iraqi weapons that could be proved to be 'threatening' US and British troops in Kuwait and inside the Kurdish safe haven in northern Iraq. Five strikes did occur against Iraqi missile launchers that were located moving outside their barracks.

WG CDR DAVE ROBERTSON
RAF Tornado navigator and commander of 617 Squadron
Ali Al Salem Airbase, Kuwait

The forty-strong detachment from the RAF's 617 'Dambusters' Squadron detachment deployed to the Gulf emirate of Kuwait in February 2003 as part of the massive American and British build-up confronting Iraq. Their new home was a huge airbase in the Kuwaiti desert, packed full of combat jets and helicopter gunships ready to join a massive air offensive should US President George Bush and British Prime Minister Tony Blair order the overthrow of Saddam Hussein.

Robertson said that his aircrew had engaged an Iraqi air defence site even before the war started, after US and British aircraft flying over Iraq 'had been threatened'.

'A target was identified and we were tasked with neutralizing it', he said. 'We went and took it out. Our attack was successful and the bomb damage assessment proved the target was destroyed.'

The controversial patrols were at the centre of a propaganda battle, with the Iraqis claiming the US and British raids had killed thousands of civilians since they had begun over a decade ago. 'We only drop [bombs] when there is no risk of collateral damage [to civilians]', said Robertson. 'Our weapons can be guided with pin-point accuracy. On several occasions we got to [the bomb] release point but were not happy that we could avoid civilians so we did not drop and brought our bombs home.'

'We know when the Iraqis make claims that we've caused civilian casualties', he said. 'On the occasions in the past when I know no weapons were released on a target, they have claimed we bombed - it was a blatant lie. I tell my wife, "Don't believe anything you read in the newspapers and only half what you see on TV."'

CAPTAIN KEVIN 'KC' ALBRIGHT
Commander Carrier Air Wing 14 - USS *Abraham Lincoln*

'We have operated here for eleven years, denying [Saddam Hussein] use of the south', said Albright in November 2002. 'We have gained significant combat experience in Operation Southern Watch. Flying over the same terrain you will fight over is a real luxury. We have gained experience shooting real missiles. Over the past eleven years we have had the advantage.'

'There are no free lunches in this business', he said. 'We have gained experience but the [Iraqis] have also gained experience.'

Albright added that every aircraft in the US and British inventories has been given substantial improvements over the past decade, including GPS navigation devices, night-vision goggles and improved weapons. 'If [war] does happen [Saddam Hussein] is going to be on the defence pretty quickly and will not recover', predicted Albright.

Surface-to-air missile (SAM) and anti-aircraft fire has 'gone up significantly', said Albright. 'They are really trying hard and are not just firing up in the air, they are firing at our people', he said.

The Iraqi air defence command had become very skilful at rapidly moving SAM and gun batteries around into populated areas to make it difficult for US and British pilots to strike at them without risking civilian casualties. Finding individual mobile SAM batteries proved 'difficult', said Albright. To counter these tactics the US and British forces developed a series of what were termed 'response options'. These were 'target menus' allowing patrolling pilots to strike at the air defence command post bunkers controlling a specific region if Iraqi air defence units under their control opened fire. Supporting radar and communications infrastructure could also be attacked.

A Royal Australian Air Force F/A-18 Hornet pilot of No. 75 Squadron is assisted with post-flight procedures by ground crew after arrival at Al Udeid Airbase in Qatar. (Australian DoD)

The 379th Air Expeditionary Wing at Al Udeid brought together US, British and Australian aircraft to form the largest strike wing in the Middle East.

USAF F-16 Fighting Falcons bore the brunt of air patrols over the northern no fly zone from 1991 until US-led forces launched their invasion of Iraq in March 2003. (US DoD/JCC(D))

US Secretary of Defense Donald H. Rumsfeld was the driving force behind US plans to attack Iraq.

(DoD photo by Helene C. Stikkel)

A chartered American Airlines 767 touches down at RAF Fairford, delivering deploying personnel for the USAF Bomber wing being stood up at the UK base.

(SSgt Jim Fisher/USAF)

A B-2 Spirit stealth bomber stands parked in front of B-52 Stratofortresses on the British Indian Ocean island of Diego Garcia.
(USAF/Senior Airman Nathan G. Bevier)

The Combined Air Operation Center (CAOC) at Prince Sultan Airbase in Saudi Arabia was the nerve centre for all US, British and Australian air activity over Iraq. (USAF)

A C-5 Galaxy delivered personnel and equipment to a base in the Middle East as part of the US build-up for the Iraq war.
(USAF/Tech. Sgt James Mossman)

Maj Gen James Amos commanded the 3rd Marine Air Wing at Ahmed Al Jaber Airbase in Kuwait. (3rd MAW PAO)

UK National Contingent Commander AM Brian Burridge led the British contribution to Operation Iraqi Freedom. (Tim Ripley)

UK Air Component Commander AVM Glenn Torpy visits RAF Tornado crews at Ali Al Salem Airbase in the run-up to war. (Tim Ripley)

The USS Abraham Lincoln (CVN 72) had three squadrons of F/A-18 Hornets embarked, VFA-25 and 113 with the F/A-18C and VFA-115 with the F/A-18E Super Hornet. The ship is operating in the northern Arabian Gulf in November 2002, while supporting Operation Southern Watch.

(Tim Ripley)

Sea King AEW Mk 7 helicopters of 849 Naval Air Squadron flew surveillance missions from HMS Ark Royal in the northern Arabian Gulf.

(Tim Ripley)

US Army Patriot missile batteries were deployed in Kuwait throughout the 1990s to defend against Iraqi missile attacks. (Tim Ripley)

47

An F-14D Tomcat is prepared for launch from the USS Abraham Lincoln (CVN 72) in the northern Arabian Gulf in November 2002, while supporting Operation Southern Watch. (Tim Ripley)

RAF Tornados are prepared for no-fly zone patrols at Ali Al Salem Airbase in March 2003. US Marine Corps and RAF helicopters also operated from the Kuwaiti base.
(Tim Ripley)

US Marine Corps F/A-18 Hornets deployed in strength to Ahmed Al Jaber Airbase in Kuwait in January and February 2003, as the 3rd Marine Air Wing prepared for Operation Iraqi Freedom. (Tim Ripley)

CHAPTER 4

Opening Attack

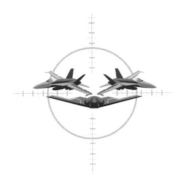

US President George Bush's 17 March 2003 deadline for Saddam Hussein and his two sons to leave Iraq forthwith set the clock ticking for war. US-led forces in the Middle East increased their readiness, reducing their notice to move time to four hours.

General Tommy Franks was ordered to be ready to launch his troops into action as soon as the ultimatum ran out. During 19 March, intelligence emerged from Baghdad that Saddam Hussein and his sons were meeting at Doura Farms on the southern outskirts of the Iraqi capital.

A series of high-level video conferences between Washington and US Central Command (CENTCOM) in Qatar were held, and eventually George Bush agreed to an attack being made to kill Saddam Hussein. It seems the prospect of killing the Iraqi president was considered just too good an opportunity to miss, even if the other elements of the main attack force were not quite ready. Gen Franks presented President Bush with the attack option and he signed off on it, allowing the US Middle East commander to give the 'go-command'.

Planning for time-sensitive targeting had been under way for a long time, with a pair of Lockheed F-117 Night Hawks of the 8th Fighter Squadron being held on alert at the giant US airbase at Al Udeid in Qatar. The F-117 pilots were given four hours until dawn broke to prepare for the mission and fly to Baghdad. The aircraft were each armed with Raytheon EGBU-27 bombs, which could be guided by both lasers and satellite guidance systems.

Although famous for its radar invisibility, one F-117 was shot down during the Kosovo war, so an 'air defence suppression package' was sent up to make sure that no Iraqi air defence crews were lucky. Grumman EA-6B Prowler jamming and Lockheed F-16CJ Fighting Falcons' suppression of enemy air defence (SEAD) aircraft also helped ease the way to Baghdad for the F-117s. A barrage of some forty Tomahawk cruise missiles was also launched against Doura Farms from four US Navy warships, the USS *Milius, Donald Cook, Bunker Hill* and *Cowpens*, and two nuclear submarines, the USS *Montpelier* and *Cheyenne*, in the Arabian Gulf and Red Sea. But although the strike was mounted with great rapidity, the Iraqi president and his sons escaped unharmed.

As the strike against Baghdad was under way, more waves of air strikes were launched on Iraqi troop positions around Basra, knocking out four radar and communications sites. Other US air strikes hit Iraqi troop positions along the Kuwaiti border, including long-range artillery near Az Zubayr, GHN-45 155 mm long-range artillery on the Al Faw peninsula and a surface-to-surface missile system near Basra to neutralize the threat to US and British troops in Kuwait.

In an apparent re-run of the 1991 Gulf War, the opening morning of Operation Iraqi Freedom saw a duel between Iraqi missiles and US Patriot anti-ballistic missile batteries. Two Ababil 100 or Al Samoud battlefield ballistic missiles were intercepted over northern Kuwait by Patriots defending US and British airfields, ports and troop concentrations in the Gulf emirate.

At least half a dozen Patriot batteries were deployed to Kuwait for just such an eventuality. They were equipped with the latest PAC-3 version of the Scud, which uses so-called 'hit-to-kill' technology, very different from the old Patriots that were used in Operation Desert Storm. One Iraqi-manufactured version of the Chinese-supplied Silkworm anti-ship guided missiles, dubbed Seersucker by the Americans, was also fired by the Iraqis, but it landed harmlessly in the desert north of Kuwait. Eventually the Iraqis would fire twelve Ababil 100s or Al Samouds and five Seersuckers at Kuwait. All the Ababils and Al Samouds that were classed as threats were intercepted, but the Seersuckers got through the Patriot defence network.

Tension within the US military was not eased by reports from the Central Intelligence Agency (CIA) that a column of ninety Iraqi tanks was heading towards the Kuwaiti border. A flight of USAF McDonnell Douglas F-15E Strike Eagles was sent to intercept the column, which turned out not to exist, but this was not before the 1st Marine Division had hurriedly reorganized its attack plan.

As a result of these attacks and intelligence that the Iraqis were about to commit acts of sabotage to destroy oil fields around Basra, General Franks considered moving forward the start of the land invasion to the evening of 20 March. This was twenty-four hours ahead of the point when the air forces would be ready to strike Baghdad, but the need to prevent what was dubbed 'environmental terrorism' led General Franks to resequence his attack plan.

US and British ground troops started advancing into southern Iraq during the evening of 20 March, capturing the Al Faw peninsula, driving to the gates of Basrah and punching 200 miles up the Euphrates valley towards Baghdad.

Helicopters played a key role in the first of these operations, lifting assault troops of the British 3 Commando Brigade into landing zones near the oil facilities on the Al Faw oil fields. US special-forces troops landed by USAF Sikorsky MH-53M Pave Lows preceded the main landings to secure the oil facilities in coup de main operations. The British Joint Helicopter Force used a force of RAF Chinooks and Pumas, Royal Navy Sea King HC4s, Army Air Corps Lynx AH7s and AH1s, supported by US Marine Corps CH-53E Sea Stallions, CH-46E Sea Knights and AH-1W Super Cobras to move the assault force. Royal Navy Sea King AEW7s and Merlin MPH1s flew top cover, co-ordinating the scores of helicopters flying in the congested air space over the northern Gulf. Tragedy struck during these operations when a USMC CH-46E carrying British Royal Marines into action crashed, killing all twelve people on board. These landings were the first phase of British operations to secure Basrah, Iraq's second city.

At the same time the 1st US Marine Divisions advanced north into the Rumailah oil fields, under air cover provided by the 3rd Marine Air Wing.

The US Army's V Corps was now pushing directly towards Baghdad with the aim of destroying the Republican Guard forces defending the southern approaches to the Iraqi capital. Bell OH-58D Kiowa Warrior scout helicopters of the 7th Cavalry ranged ahead of the 3rd Infantry Division as it pushed past Nasiriyah, seized Talill Airbase on 22 March and then pressed on to Najaf, only a hundred miles from Baghdad. V Corps began massing around Najaf, with work beginning on forward bases for attack helicopters and Patriot anti-missile batteries being brought up. A runway for Hunter unmanned aerial vehicles was also built near Najaf to allow them to find targets for 11th Aviation Brigade's Boeing AH-64D Longbow Apaches.

Following up behind V Corps, the 1st Marine Division reached Nasiriyah during 23 March, and soon found itself locked into a series of ambushes and skirmishes. Bell AH-1W Super Cobras were called up to provide close air support, but the fighting was so intense that fixed-wing aircraft were called in. There was another tragic mishap when a USAF Fairchild A-10A Warthog hit a Marine convoy by accident and nine Americans died. The casualties during the battle were heavy, with fifteen Marines dying and more than one hundred wounded. This overwhelmed the Marines' casualty evacuation systems, and there were not enough Bell UH-1N Hueys or CH-46Es to fly out the wounded.

US, British and Australian air forces provided extensive air support for these operations, but there were few military targets of any significance in southern Iraq. The regular Iraqi army seemed to melt away into the cities, and paramilitary forces provided the main opposition to US-led forces.

Apart from the US Marines' CH-46E and a USAF special forces MH-53M, the only aircraft lost so far were two Westland Sea King AEW7s that collided over the northern Gulf, killing all seven crewmen, and an RAF Panavia Tornado GR4 shot down accidentally by a US Patriot missile battery in Kuwait, with the loss of two crewmen.

WG CDR DAVID PROWSE
Commanding Officer 18 Squadron RAF - HMS *Ark Royal*

Off Iraq's southern coastline Chinook helicopter pilots of 18 Squadron led the largest air assault operation since the Vietnam War to land Royal Marines on the Al Faw peninsula. Their target was key oil facilities, where supporters of the Iraqi leader were threatening to flood the Arabian Gulf with millions of barrels of oil in an act of 'environmental terrorism'.

Prowse led the first wave of four twin-rotor Chinooks into action that night, flying at 100 feet through dust storms using night-vision goggles. Apart from some tracer fire 'whizzing around', he described the delivery of the first wave of Royal Marines as 'fairly unremarkable'. He went on,

'The second and third waves were more interesting. We had troops inside and underslung loads. One Land Rover inside and one outside. We were at max weight, flying at 100 feet over Bubiyan island. The visibility was zero, wind picked up the dust and muck from artillery fire thrown up into the air. We could not see ground or other aircraft so we went into unplanned holding patterns until the weather cleared. The landing zone was too hot for us to approach. The [controller] on ground tried to call us in between enemy activity. They were trying to prepare another landing site by blowing up telephone poles so we could get down on road. That's what delayed the second wave [of helicopters]. The third wave then had to hold off between mortaring on the landing zone.

Then after that we moved part of the landing force, then switched to off-loading HMS *Ark Royal* and HMS *Ocean* of [the Marines'] vehicles. That carried on for next two days. We flew just short of 100 hours on five aircraft, continuous wave of aircraft, swapping crews around.

What was unique was the air assault, I've never seen helicopters used so aggressively in a plan. Every one and all the aircraft came out unscathed, an excellent experience. When I first briefed my inner circle on the plan there was stunned silence, after two months' training everyone was ready for it. In the end the plan changed very little, it flew as briefed to me. We knew the risks, that gave us a confidence level.'

CALLSIGN 'DEADLY'

US Marine Corps Bell AH-1W Cobra Pilot and Operations Officer
Marine Light/Attack Helicopter Squadron 269

Our flight of four flew north [from our base in Kuwait] and reached the release point. The four-ship split up into two two-aircraft elements (a flight of two is called a section . . . two sections make a division). My section went to the right. My commanding officer's section went to the left. We proceed to our firing points. Upon arrival, Kujo is working the FLIR (Forward Looking Infra-Red) sensor to find our assigned targets. Unfortunately, the target area photos didn't quite display all the surrounding terrain features that were in the FLIR's field of view. What seemed like hours for Kujo to pick out the right targets, actually only took about a minute or two. As I'm sitting in this hover, waiting for Kujo to find the targets, I look down to my right side. On my night-vision goggles (NVGs), I can see a Kuwaiti family outside their house, looking up into the sky, and watching the 'fireworks' show. Kujo locates the targets . . . three missiles away. Border post destroyed. Thank God that's over with.

After the initial border-post strikes, my section proceeds to a FARP (Forward Arming and Refuelling Point) that had been set up only hours prior near the Iraq/Kuwait border. None of us had been there before. The FARP was located on an asphalt road . . . but there were power lines and sand all over the place. Just to land for gas took me four attempts. I kept having to wave off because of the lack of visibility. Not being able to land because of visibility had never happened to me before. I'm fighting panic and despair. We're just about out of gas. Finally with Kujo's help, we make it safe on deck. After refuelling, we shut down and assumed a strip alert.

Patriot missile launchers of Battery C, 2nd Battalion, 1st Air Defense Artillery Regiment, deployed to Kuwait to defend against Iraqi missile attacks, were equipped with the new PAC-3 version of the weapon.
(US Central Command)

Two CH-47 Chinook helicopters head north from Camp Udairi in northern Kuwait toward Iraq, carrying soldiers with the 3rd Battalion, 101st Aviation Regiment, 101st Airborne Division, to set up a forward fuel resupply point to allow the division to conduct further air assaults deep into Iraq.

(US Army/Pfc James Matise)

AH-64 Apache helicopters wait on the flight line at Camp Udairi in northern Kuwait as a group of UH-60 Black Hawk helicopters fly over, carrying the infantry troops from 187th Infantry Regiment, 101st Airborne Division into southern Iraq.

(US Army/Pfc James Matise)

CH-47 Chinook helicopter crews of the 101st Airborne Division are seen on the flight line at Camp Udairi in northern Kuwait shortly before flying across the border into Iraq.

(US Army/Pfc James Matise)

An F-117 Night Hawk of the 8th Expeditionary Fighter Squadron based at Al Udeid Airbase in Qatar dropped the first bombs of Operation Iraqi Freedom in the early hours of 20 March.

(USAF Staff Sgt Derrick C. Goode)

Iraq responded to US air strikes on Baghdad by firing Al Samoud 2 missiles at US and British bases in northern Kuwait. (USMC)

Boeing Chinook HC2s of 18 Squadron RAF flying from HMS Ark Royal off the Kuwaiti coast carried the first waves of Royal Marines to land on the Al Faw peninsula. (Tim Ripley)

RAF BAe Harrier GR7s flying from Ahmed Al Jaber Airbase, Kuwait, were in the air during the first day of the war to provide close air support for British and US troops along the border with Iraq.
(Tim Ripley)

A USMC UH-1 Huey lands next to a US Marine Corps column as it moves north into Iraq.
(USMC/Lance Cpl Andrew P. Roufs)

A Merlin MPH Mk1 helicopter lands on HMS Ark Royal off the Kuwaiti coast during a surveillance patrol to monitor Iraqi naval activity in the crowded Arabian Gulf.
(Tim Ripley)

A US Marine Corps CH-46 Sea Knight flies over the streets of Nasiriyah, where US troops ran into serious resistance during the opening weekend of the war. (USMC)

Sea King AEW Mk 7 helicopters of 849 Naval Air Squadron based on HMS Ark Royal monitored air movement in the northern Arabian Gulf

(Tim Ripley)

Sea King HC4 helicopters embarked on HMS Ocean formed the heavy-lift element of the Commando Helicopter Force for the assault on the Al Faw peninsula.
(Tim Ripley)

F/A-18 Hornet strike fighters of the 3rd US Marine Corps Air Wing operating from Ahmed Al Jaber Airbase, Kuwait, were heavily tasked to support the initial drive by US and British ground troops across the border in Iraq.
(Tim Ripley)

Iraqi-made versions of the Chinese Silkworm anti-ship missiles, dubbed Seersuckers, were fired at US and British troops in Kuwait in response to American air raids on Baghdad on 20 March.
(US DoD/JCC(D))

Ali Al Salem Airbase in northern Kuwait was a major hub for US and British air activity in the opening days of the war. Here an RAF Tornado is being overflown by US Marine Corps CH-46 Sea Knight helicopters, and in the background is a USAF C-130 Hercules.
(Tim Ripley)

CHAPTER 5

Strategic Air Campaign

The next phase of the US-led onslaught on Iraq was the strategic air campaign, which began to unfold around Baghdad from the evening of 21 March. The aim of the strike was to cripple the Iraqi government in a series of huge air and missile strikes. In the space of a few hours the majority of Saddam Hussein's palaces, security operations, intelligence services and Ba'ath Party buildings in Baghdad were to be hit.

These targets were concentrated in the centre of downtown Baghdad in an area within view of the international media's camera positions on the roof of the Iraqi Ministry of Information. The dramatic footage was broadcast live around the world, and the evening became immortalized as the 'shock and awe' night.

The concentration of targets was deliberate, and it was hoped the attack would dramatically 'decapitate' the Iraqi government by killing its senior leadership. If they could not be killed, then it was hoped the attack would severely disrupt their ability to co-ordinate resistance and scare Saddam Hussein and his top lieutenants into fleeing the capital.

The USA was also sending a 'message' to the Iraqi population and military, in the hope that they would change sides and stop supporting the government.

'We wanted to make it clear to the Iraqi people that we were attacking regime targets', said USAF Col Mace Carpenter, chief strategist at the CAOC. 'We wanted them to see that we were clearly targeting those people who had been repressing them.'

To achieve the desired effect, hundreds of strike aircraft were to be employed in the 'shock and awe' effort that would last for seventy-two hours, which would see the employment of some 2,500 individual bombs and cruise missiles. Stealth Lockheed F-117 Night Hawks and Northrop Grumman B-2 Spirits led the air assault into Baghdad, along with hundreds of stand-off weapons, including Raytheon BGM-109 Tomahawk Land Attack Missiles (TLAM), Boeing AGM-86C/D Conventional Air-Launched Cruise Missiles (CALCM), MBDA Storm Shadows and Raytheon AGM-154 Joint Stand-off Weapons (JSOW).

To fight through the air defences around Baghdad, hundreds more suppression-of-enemy-air-defence (SEAD) aircraft were launched against surface-to-air missile (SAM) batteries, radar sites, communications nodes and command bunkers of the Iraqi Air Defence Command. The predominantly US SEAD force was backed up by British Tornado GR4 aircraft firing the new Storm Shadow cruise missile fitted with BROACH penetrating warheads, which were used to destroy hardened air defence command bunkers. US Navy BGM-34 Firebee drones were launched over Baghdad to drop chaff corridors to confuse Iraqi radars. Scores of AGM-141 Tactical Air-Launched Decoys (TALDs) were fired to try to force the Iraqis to switch on radars, allowing them to be targeted by US Raytheon AGM-88 High-Speed Anti-radiation Missiles and British BAe Dynamics ALARM missiles.

Supporting this huge air armada would require a major effort by US and British air refuelling tankers to ensure all the strike jets reached their targets with a full weapon load.

Many of the targets in and around Baghdad were studied extensively prior to the war, but the CAOC staff kept them constantly under review and incorporated new targets as they emerged or as old ones were found to be invalid. This process continued even as the attack was under way, in co-operation with the CAOC's time-sensitive targeting cell. Out of some 2,124 'regime leadership' targets nominated for attack, only 1,779 were eventually bombed by the end of the war.

The first 'shock and awe' strikes went off with no US or British air losses after the Iraqi 'super missile engagement zone' (MEZ) failed to live up to expectations. 'We had been led to believe that venturing into the 'super MEZ' meant certain death', commented one British pilot.

Even as CAOC officers watched television broadcasts live from Baghdad on 'shock and awe' night, their attention had moved to rolling out further air strikes against Iraqi strategic targets.

For the remainder of the war, strike aircraft and missiles were used to hit leadership targets in Baghdad and elsewhere in Iraq. This also required a constant effort to hunt down and destroy what remained of the Iraqi Air Defence Command. This resulted in a 'cat and mouse' game between US and British SEAD forces and the Iraqi missile crews, as the latter tried to hide their diminishing assets from detection.

Each evening, fixed-wing strike aircraft made forays into the Baghdad 'super MEZ' to hit targets such as palaces, telephone exchanges and security headquarters. Cruise missiles took up the strain during daytime. These strikes remained a mix of pre-planned raids and missions against targets of opportunity revealed by intelligence. Eventually some fifty time-sensitive leadership targets were attacked, along with 102 associated with weapons of mass destruction and four designated as 'terrorist' related.

Iraqi resistance to US and British air offensives was at first furious as hundreds of SAMs and thousands of anti-aircraft artillery (AAA) pieces were fired at the attacking aircraft. After the first few days of the air offensive against Baghdad the level of resistance began to diminish, until the commander of the Iraqi Air Defence Command was sacked and his replacement re-energized his forces. In total during the war, the Iraqis fired some 1,660 SAMs, with 1,224 'AAA events' and 436 radar illuminations being recorded by US, British and Australian airmen. Although there were some close

shaves, the Iraqi Air Defence Command failed to shoot down a single US, British or Australian aircraft with any of its radar-guided SAMs.

The Iraqi Air Force proved equally ineffective at putting up resistance to the US-led airborne onslaught. No Iraqi fighters took to the skies during the war. It seems that the Iraqi Air Force commanders before the war ordered their squadrons to disperse into the countryside to hide their aircraft from US surveillance efforts. Iraqi aircraft were towed off airbases and hidden in palm groves, industrial complexes and residential areas. Some aircraft were even buried in sand.

The exact reasons for this strategy are unclear. It could either have been an effort to preserve their assets until after the war was over, or that US attacks on the Iraqi communications systems prevented counter-attack orders getting through to front-line pilots. Given the 'top-down' nature of the Baghdad regime, initiative was unsurprisingly not in large supply among Iraq's airmen.

The strategic air campaign proved to be remarkably limited in scope and intensity compared to Operation Desert Storm, with just under 1,500 regime leadership targets being attacked. Efforts to neutralize the Iraqi air force and air defences were also limited with 1,441 'air supremacy' targets being attacked. Unlike the 1991 conflict, there was no systematic effort to destroy the Iraqi airbase infrastructure of hardened aircraft shelters, beyond the cratering of a number of runways. A further 832 strikes were made against targets that were believed to be associated with weapons of mass destruction.

The civilian infrastructure of Iraq was also not attacked, and up to the point when US ground troops approached the capital, Baghdad's power and water remained on. The buzzword among US and British air planners was 'effects-based warfare'. This emphasized the effect of an air attack, rather than just physical destruction. The chaotic and disorganized nature of Iraqi resistance to US-led ground offensives is seen by US and British commanders as proof that its strategic air campaign effectively paralysed the ability of the Iraqis to fight back. Until insiders from Saddam Hussein's inner circle give their side of the war it will be difficult to truly judge the success of the air campaign against Baghdad.

LT-COL TOM BERGY

Commander, 524th Fighter Squadron - Ali Al Salem Airbase Kuwait

'We are a multi-role fighter squadron and we deployed here in December for Operation Southern Watch and then we stayed and transitioned to Operation Iraqi Freedom.

Our primary function was the use of precision-guided munitions. We are the only F-16CG squadron in theatre. We flew with AIM-120 and nine air-to-air missiles, LANTIRN targeting pod, Paveway laser-guided bombs and Joint Direct Attack Munition (JDAM), dumb bombs - Mk 82 and 84s - and cluster bomb units (CBU.)

We did just about everything, Defensive Counter Air (DCA), strategic attack on "shock and awe" night and, as the ground force moved forward, we transitioned to kill box operations, interdiction, close air support and dropping psychological leaflets. We were multi-role, multifaceted.

First night stood out, we flew north-east of Baghdad - close to the downtown super missile engagement zone - hitting at air defences. The Iraqis still had formidable air defences.

For a lot of my guys this is the first time in combat, they did an outstanding job. This was every squadron commander's dream.'

WG CDR 'MOOSE' POOLE

RAF Tornado pilot and commander of II (AC) Squadron - Ali Al Salem Airbase, Kuwait

'As we pressed north, radars on and warning receivers showing little activity, we watched the bombing of Baghdad. Explosions under the cloud cover looked like the sort of light show that Jean Michelle Jarre might use, only this outdoor concert wasn't at Houston. Imaging the sound track, we watched missiles streak into the air in a volley of desperation, blindly hoping to find a Coalition aircraft.

After what seemed like eons, we reached the target. Always a tense place to be, the simplest of tasks become so difficult as you struggle to funnel and restrain the adrenaline and get on with the job in hand. The training in the RAF is second to none and boy do you depend on what has become instinct when the enemy are shooting at you. There is no time to think what needs to be done, you need to do it automatically - it is an art, not a science.

We proceeded to pepper the target with precision strikes against carefully calculated pressure points - I was not surprised to see the Iraqis respond, albeit in vain. Their missiles were never going to reach us but it takes some self-convincing at the time, as you watch the mesmerizing glow of each rocket motor eventually fade. Willing the jet higher and faster, we took what seemed to be an eternity to egress. We were vulnerable up here, should they be bold enough to launch fighters against us, and while we had cover around, it would take a few minutes to reach us. That threat thankfully never materialized and we slogged our way home, hoping the engines would continue to put up with the strain.'

This US Navy DC-130A Hercules was forward based at Ali Al Salem Airbase in Kuwait launched BGM-34 Firebee drones to drop chaff over Baghdad to confuse Iraq's air defences.
(Northrop Grumman)

F-16CJs from the 22nd Expeditionary Fighter Squadron and the 157th EFS of South Carolina Air National Guard await take-off clearance from Al Udeid Airbase in Qatar to fly suppression-of-enemy-air-defence missions.
(USAF/SMSgt Edward Snyder)

F-15C Eagles of the 1st Fighter Wing flew round-the-clock combat air patrols to keep Iraqi aircraft on the ground and to protect friendly 'high-value' assets.
(USAF/MSgt Mark Bucher)

Air commanders and staff at the Combined Air Operation Center (CAOC) at Prince Sultan Airbase in Saudi Arabia were able to monitor all air activity over the Middle East on computer-generated maps, projected onto large screens.
(USAF/Sgt Derrick Goodie)

The scene at Diego Garcia while other aircraft of the 40th Air Expeditionary Wing prepare to launch for missions against Iraq.
(USAF/Senior Airman Nathan G. Bevier)

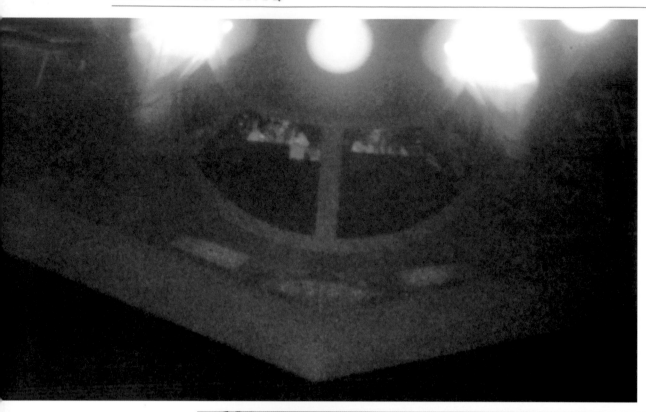

A B-2 Spirit stealth bomber of the 393rd Expeditionary Bomb Squadron refuels at night before penetrating into Iraqi air space. The B-2s and F-117s were the only aircraft to operate over Baghdad's 'super' missile engagement zone in the opening hours of the war.
(US DoD/JCC(D))

Bomb artwork on Paveway laser-guided bomb on the wing of an F-16CG Fighting Falcon of the 524th Fighter Squadron at Ahmed Al Jaber Airbase, Kuwait.
(Tim Ripley)

Mission markings on an F-16CG Fighting Falcon of the 524th Fighter Squadron at Ahmed Al Jaber Airbase, Kuwait.
(Tim Ripley)

F-16CG Fighting Falcons of the 524th Fighter Squadron were part of a combat wing of more than 100 combat aircraft based at Ahmed Al Jaber Airbase, Kuwait.
(Tim Ripley)

US Marine Corps F/A-18 Hornets based at Ahmed Al Jaber Airbase, Kuwait, also joined the strategic air offensive against Iraq. (Tim Ripley)

An Australian F/A-18C Hornet fighter pilot of No. 75 Squadron checks behind during his preparations for take-off from Al Udeid Airbase in Qatar. (Australian DoD)

A 617 Squadron RAF badge worn by a Tornado GR4 pilot at Ali Al Salem Airbase, Kuwait.

(Tim Ripley)

USS Porter *fires a Tomahawk Land Attack Missile at Iraq on 23 March, as part of a campaign that eventually saw more than 800 of the cruise missiles fired at targets in Iraq by US and British ships and submarines.*
(US DoD/JCC(D))

Paveway laser-guided and JDAM and satellite-guided bombs about to be loaded onto jets of the 3rd US Marine Corps Air Wing at Ahmed Al Jaber Airbase, Kuwait.

(Tim Ripley)

SPECIAL SECURITY OFFICES, BAGHDAD
POST STRIKE

*Post-strike bomb damage assessment imagery of
the Iraqi Special Security Offices in Baghdad.* (US DoD)

REGIME VIP FACILITY, TIKRIT
POST STRIKE

YN692693

REGIME C2 SITE, IRAQ
POST STRIKE

Post-strike bomb damage assessment imagery of a presidential palace complex in Tikrit, Saddam Hussein's home town. (US DoD)

Post-strike bomb damage assessment imagery of a headquarters building in Baghdad. (US DoD)

A US Navy F-14 Tomcat at speed during a fly-by of its carrier. (US DoD/JCC(D))

An F-117 of the 8th Expeditionary Fighter Squadron leads a pair of F-15Es of the 4th Fighter Wing out onto the runway at Al Udeid Airbase in Qatar before heading north to attack Iraq. (USAF/Staff Sgt Derrick C. Goode)

CHAPTER 6

The Enablers

The air campaign against Iraq was only possible because of an array of specialist support aircraft - command and control, reconnaissance, surveillance, air refuelling and airlift.

While the 'strikers' or 'bomb-dropping' aircraft may have stolen the limelight during Operation Iraqi Freedom, more than two-thirds of all participating aircraft were specialist support machines, or 'enablers'.

In the 1991 Gulf War, intelligence, surveillance and reconnaissance (ISR) aircraft had limited ability to transmit any intelligence they had collected to ground-based command posts and strike aircraft. By 2003 the US and British forces had installed high-capacity datalinks on their ISR platforms to allow intelligence to be downloaded 'live' or in real-time. Out of the 41,404 sorties flown during the war, some 1,683 were by ISR aircraft.

The aim was to provide commanders in the CAOC with real-time intelligence on what was happening in the air and on the ground throughout Iraq and neighbouring countries. The fusion of this information into air, land and sea 'pictures' projected onto computer screens was the key to allowing senior US commanders to make rapid decisions about the tasking of strike aircraft. The world's largest ever tactical datalink network then ensured that every user - in the air, on the ground or at sea - connected to the network could view these 'pictures'.

At the heart of generating the 'air picture' was the Boeing E-3 Sentry AWACS radar aircraft. The USAF's fifteen E-3Cs and RAF's four E-3Ds in the Middle East were airborne '24/7' over Iraq and neighbouring airspace in a series of orbits to ensure total coverage of the operational theatre. Their radar returns were down-

loaded in real time to CAOC and other command posts in the Middle East to allow commanders to watch the air war unfold. Icons on the 'air picture' display showed the position of every friendly and Iraqi aircraft, as well as civilian traffic. An airborne 'battle staff' was also embarked on each E-3 to allow controllers to finesse the final execution of the hundreds of US, British and Australian aircraft flying into Iraqi air space. Controllers on the AWACS were also a key link with the ground forces, allocating individual strike aircraft to attack close-air-support targets nominated by forward air controllers.

The US Navy's twenty carrier-borne Northrop Grumman E-2C Hawkeyes added to the 'air picture' and also filled in gaps in AWACS coverage, flying some 442 missions during the war.

The job of monitoring Iraqi air defence activity and communications traffic was the job of the USAF Boeing RC-135 River Joint, RAF BAe Nimrod R.1 and US Navy Lockheed EP-3 Aries III. These 'hoovered' Iraqi radar signals and communications traffic and, in real time, downloaded them to the CAOC and AWACS. Fusion technology then displayed the information as 'threat' icons on the air picture.

To give the ground force commanders the same level of 'situational awareness' as their air force counterparts, seven Northrop Grumman E-8C Joint STARS ground surveillance aircraft were used extensively during the Iraq War. They maintained continuous orbits over Iraq to provide total coverage of the battlefield, and used the moving target indicator (MTI) radar to identify the movement of Iraqi tanks, missile launchers and other military equipment in all weathers or at night. Ground commanders then merged the JSTARS radar returns with the Blue Forces Tracking satellite-based location system, fitted to all US and British vehicles, to produce the 'land picture'. When sand storms engulfed the advance on Baghdad, JSTARS was the only way US ground commanders could ensure the Iraqis did not use the bad weather to move forces to counter-attack. Some 1,700 hours of MTI radar coverage were recorded during the war.

The USAF E-3C and E-8D fleet flew some 432 missions during the war, along with 112 missions by RAF E-3Ds. To support them, US Marine Corps Lockheed KC-130 (DASC-A) airborne command post aircraft flew some seventy-five missions, co-ordinating the efforts of 3rd Marine Air Wing strike aircraft.

While the platforms that contributed the air, land and naval pictures provided the means for senior commanders to manage the battle, the information they gathered was often not in itself good enough to allow air attacks to be launched, because of the need to avoid civilian casualties or confirm target identification. This was the job of specific intelligence collection platforms, particularly imagery intelligence aircraft. These collected information needed to plan future strike missions or to confirm targets for 'time-sensitive' attack. Still imagery was the primary means of providing the former type of intelligence, and video imagery predominated in time-sensitive targeting. The level of effort put into collecting imagery intelligence can be gauged from the fact that US, British and Australian ISR aircraft collected some 42,000 still battlefield images and 3,200 hours of video imagery during the war.

USAF Lockheed U-2S Dragon Ladies and RAF English Electric Canberra PR9s were the main strategic still imagery collection platforms, and were used to maintain orbits over western, northern and southern Iraq throughout the war. They could also download imagery in real time to CAOC if necessary. A single Northrop Grumman RQ-4 Global Hawk unmanned aerial vehicle (UAV) was also used in the strategic reconnaissance role, maintaining an orbit over Baghdad and central Iraq for much of the war.

These strategic platforms were augmented extensively in the collection of still imagery by British, US Marine Corps and US Navy tactical reconnaissance (tact recce) aircraft. These BAe Tornado GR4s, BAe Harrier GR7s, McDonnell Douglas F/A-18D Hornets and Grumman F-14 Tomcats all used pod systems to photograph Iraqi targets, often going to low level to achieve tactical surprise.

Moving video imagery was the preserve of four main platforms - the USAF General Atomics RQ-1 Predator UAVs, US Army IAI/TRW RQ5 Hunter UAVs, US Marine Corps IAI/TRW RQ-2B Pioneer UAVs and US Navy

Lockheed P-3C (AIP) Orions. These had real-time datalinks to allow their imagery to be downloaded into the CAOC or ground forces command post. This capability was highly prized and allowed time-sensitive targeting to be undertaken in a way that dramatically affected ground operations.

The P-3s were particularly popular with ground commanders because their large size, long endurance and extensive communications meant that senior ground forces officers could be carried, in order to speed up the co-ordination of air strikes against targets identified by the Orion's electro-optical vision systems. Both the British and Australians used the BAe Nimrod MR2s and Orions in similar roles to support ground forces operations, but because they lacked the ability to download video in real time, they had to rely on verbal reporting over radio links.

Uniquely among the UAVs employed in the Iraq war, the Predator could be armed with either AGM-114 Hellfire laser-guided missiles or Raytheon AIM-9 Sidewinder air-to-air missiles. These allowed it to rapidly engage any targets discovered, and made it the 'weapon of choice' for time-sensitive targeting.

All senior air commanders involved in the Iraq War reported that the most important aircraft for their ability to conduct 'high temp' operations were the 268 air-to-air refuelling tankers in the Middle East. Without the tankers, no tactical aircraft or bombers would have been able to reach targets deep in Iraq, and the ISR fleet would have been limited to fleeting missions over hostile territory. The tankers were constantly used to fill orbits around Iraq's borders, so that 'inbound' strike aircraft could top off their tanks before heading for their targets. When the advance on Baghdad reached its climax in early April, a tanker orbit was set up over the Iraqi capital so that close-air-support aircraft could remain constantly on station ready to protect US troops. Even though the tanker fleet passed more than 417 million litres of fuel, there were never enough tankers to go around, and battle staff in the CAOC or on AWACS aircraft were constantly varying the operations of the tankers, often at the last minute, to ensure that aircraft assigned to high-priority missions had the fuel they needed. This was particularly demanding when time-sensitive targets emerged and jets attacking them needed fuel at short notice.

The tankers also supported the airlift fleet, refuelling aircraft flying direct from the USA or Europe with high-priority cargos. The airdrop missions into Iraq by Boeing C-17 Globemasters were also only possible thanks to air refuelling.

Airlift was a key element of the US invasion plan, and

the USAF, RAF and RAAF deployed more than 120 Lockheed C-130 aircraft to the Middle East to support the movement and resupply of ground troops. The USAF and RAF also moved scores of C-17s to bases in southern and central Europe to support the war.

As US ground troops advanced into Iraq, following up behind were specialist teams who rapidly opened up abandoned Iraqi airfields and turned them into forward operating bases (FOB) for close-air-support aircraft, airlifters and helicopters. The USAF used its contingency response groups for this task, and US Marine Corps aviation support units were also used for this mission. Many of these FOBs were within range of Iraqi artillery, so air operations had to be conducted largely at night to ensure the protection of slow-flying airlifters landing at them.

During the war some 7,413 airlift sorties were flown by USAF C-130s and C-17s, which, when compared to the 8,828 fighter missions flown by the USAF, illustrates the level of activity of the airlift force. Some 9,962 passengers were moved, and more than 12,000 tons of cargo were carried, by the USAF airlifters alone.

Operation Iraqi Freedom showed yet again the vital role played by 'enabling' aircraft. Not only did they play a key role in finding targets and co-ordinating strike missions, but refuelling and airlift efforts ensured that the pace and tempo of the US-led onslaught was unrelenting.

WG CDR HARRY HALLETT
Commander RAF E-3D Sentry Detachment - Prince Sultan Airbase, Saudi Arabia

Four RAF Boeing E-3Ds Sentry AWACS aircraft from 8 and 13 Squadrons flew out to a desert airbase from RAF Waddington in Lincolnshire immediately before the war to work alongside their USAF colleagues, who already had fifteen AWACS ready to co-ordinate the air offensive. Wg-Cdr Hallett described a typical mission:

'Down the back of the aircraft is a busy place to be. Controllers are not leaving their seats for hours at a time, food and drink has to be brought to them as they can't move from the tasking. The sheer scale of the number of Coalition aircraft involved has to be seen to be fully appreciated. When you consider they are flying operational missions, it is all the more impressive. We are averaging 12 hours a trip, with air-to-air refuelling halfway through the mission. A few missions have to be extended to 13-14 hours when tasking has demanded it. We have the ability to refuel from British and American tankers, with their respective probe-and-drogue and boom systems. As good as they all are, we find the American KC-135 tanker particularly useful in its ability to deliver fuel at speed. Many of the crews out here have only just left the Afghanistan commitment. Before that, there was Kosovo, and before that, there was Bosnia. A lot of personnel on detachment have served all three of those, so it gives you an indication of the expertise we can call upon.'

LT-COL GARY FABRICIUS
15th Expeditionary Reconnaissance Squadron - Ali Al Salem Airbase Kuwait

'We played a very significant role in the prosecuting of the war against the Iraqi regime, not just against the military but the regime itself.

We provide eyes on the battlefield for Coalition air and land component commanders, giving them eyes on battlespace so they could make informed decisions with real-time analysis. From day one, Predator was a pure intelligence, surveillance and reconnaissance (ISR) platform and has since moved to next major step, destroying time-sensitive targets.

We now do find, fix, track, target, engage and assess on a single platform, we do the entire mission. We have taken what used to be done in hours down to minutes and never put aircrew in danger. This is a significantly changed mission. We locate enemy weapons systems, identify what it is, especially in relation to mobile targets, follow, track and then engage it with Hellfire missiles.

We do not necessarily employ our own weapons. We do targeting for other platforms, by laser designation or talking them on to target. We have RQ ISR version and MQ weapons capable version of the Predator.

We can pass strike co-ordinates, use video to talk to aircraft commanders, passing information to pilots. We are similar to an airborne forward air controller but are only qualified for certain types of close air support missions.'

An Australian C-130H Hercules of No. 36 Squadron is marshalled into a parking bay at Doha International Airport in Qatar, where it joined a USAF air transport wing.
(Australian DoD)

USAF NKC-135 electronic intelligence-gathering aircraft based at Souda Bay on Crete operated around Iraq's borders to detect radio traffic. (US DoD/JCC(D))

E-8C JSTARS surveillance aircraft were airborne round the clock to give ground commanders constant intelligence on Iraqi troop movements. (US DoD/JCC(D))

The ramp at Rhein Main Airbase in Frankfurt, Germany, became a key hub for USAF airlifters supporting the war against Iraq. (US DoD/JCC(D))

KC-10 Extender tankers bore the brunt of the USAF's air-to-air refuelling effort during the war. (USAF/Staff Sgt Cherie A. Thurlby)

A US Navy P-3C Orion patrol aircraft based at Ali Al Salem Airbase in Kuwait provided ground commanders with real-time video imagery of key parts of the Iraqi battlefield. (USAF/Staff Sgt Tony Tolley)

An MQ-1 Predator unmanned aerial vehicle armed with a Hellfire missile awaits the call to action at Ali Al Salem Airbase in Kuwait. (USAF/Capt John Sheets)

USAF E-3 AWACS aircraft deployed to the 363rd Air Expeditionary Wing at Prince Sultan Airbase in Saudi Arabia flew round-the-clock missions to control the thousands of US, British and Australian aircraft flying into Iraqi airspace on a daily basis during the war. They also provided a vital link to ground troops in need of air support.

(USAF/Staff Sgt Matthew Hannen)

C-2A Greyhounds of VRC-40 provided logistic support for the USS Theodore Roosevelt operating in the eastern Mediterranean from RAF Akrotiri on Cyrpus.
(US Navy/Phillip A. Nickerson Jr)

A US Navy crewman on an SH-60F Sea Hawk of HS-7 photographs civilian naval traffic in the eastern Mediterranean near the USS Harry S. Truman.
(US Navy/Photographer's Mate 1st Class Michael W. Pendergrass)

A P-3C AIP Orion of VP-46 returns to Ali Al Salam Airbase in Kuwait after a mission monitoring Iraqi troop movements around Baghdad.
(US Navy/Photographer's Mate Airman Chris Otsen)

A U-2S Dragon Lady of the 9th Reconnaissance Squadron takes off from Prince Sultan Airbase, Saudi Arabia, for a surveillance mission over Iraq.
(USAF/Staff Sgt Matthew Hannen)

Battle management staff on board E-8C JSTARS surveillance aircraft were able to monitor Iraqi and friendly troop movements in real time. The imagery was downloaded to US headquarters throughout the Middle East. (USAF/Sue Sapp)

The US Central Command commander, Gen Tommy Franks, used this C40 to fly around the Middle East for meetings with his subordinate commanders or to visit his troops. (US DoD/JCC(D))

The USAF's 64th Air Expeditionary Wing at Doha International Airport, Qatar, was one of a series of air transport hubs set up to move personnel and material around the Middle East. (Tim Ripley)

BGM-34 Firebee drones were launched from US Navy DC-130A Hercules on missions to distribute chaff to confuse Iraqi defences or to deliver supplies to US special-forces teams. (Northrop Grumman)

USAF HC-130 Hercules air refuelling tankers of the 920th Rescue Group were based at Ahmed Al Jaber Airbase, Kuwait, to refuel HH-60 Pave Hawk helicopters providing combat search and rescue cover over southern Iraq. (Tim Ripley)

US Navy MH-53E Sea Dragons of HM-14 were deployed to the Arabian Gulf for mine-clearing work, and also found themselves pressed into service for logistic support tasks.

(US DoD/JCC(D))

P-3C Orions of the US Navy and the Royal Australian Air Force's Orions from No. 92 Wing provided real-time surveillance of Iraq's coast line, including Umm Qasr port as seen here, before and during the invasion, with the imagery being downloaded direct to US and British headquarters from US Navy aircraft.

(Australian DoD)

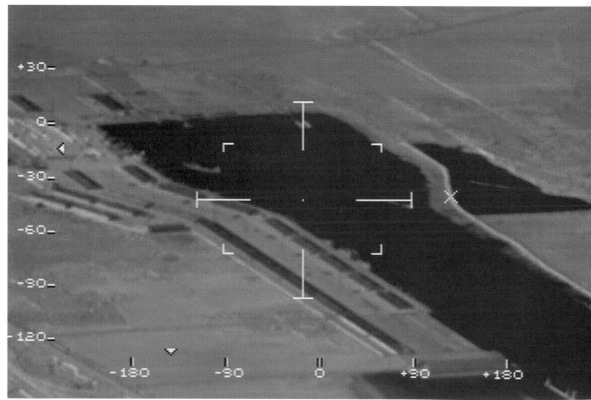

British Army Phoenix unmanned aerial vehicles of the 32nd Regiment Royal Artillery were in action throughout the siege of Basrah monitoring Iraqi troop movements. Four were lost to hostile fire. (Tim Ripley)

RQ-2 Pioneer unmanned aerial vehicles of VMU-2 flew surveillance support for US Marine Corps units advancing on Baghdad. (USMC)

Lt-Col Gary Fabricius, commander of the 15th Expeditionary Reconnaissance Squadron, the RQ-1 Predator unmanned aerial vehicle unit at Ali Al Salem Airbase, Kuwait. (Tim Ripley)

The 15th Expeditionary Reconnaissance Squadron sign is seen at Ali Al Salem Airbase, Kuwait. (Tim Ripley)

RQ-4 Global Hawk unmanned aerial vehicles supplemented the USAF's U-2S Dragon Lady fleet during the strategic reconnaissance campaign. (USAF)

RAF VC-10 tankers are engulfed in a dust storm at Prince Sultan Airbase in Saudi Arabia, from where they supported US and British aircraft attacking targets in Iraq. (US DoD/JCC(D))

CHAPTER 7
Special Forces

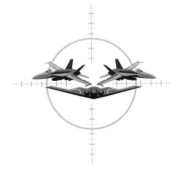

Western Iraq is a barren desert region, thinly populated by Arab tribes who make a living from herding cattle. The region, however, is one of the most strategic in the Middle East because it is the only part of Iraq from where Scud ballistic missiles could be launched at Israel. The dual-carriageway road from Baghdad to the Jordanian capital, Amman, which runs through the region, was also the main route to the outside world for the sanction-busting trade by the Iraqis.

Neutralizing a repeat of Iraqi Scud missile attacks on Israel was a high priority for Gen Franks, and he made preparations to neutralize the threat as he developed his war plans. Attention quickly focused on Jordan, which was identified as a key base to mount raids into western Iraq to prevent the region being used as a missile launch pad. This task was assigned to US Central Command's special operations component, and its commander, Brig-Gen Gary Harrell, made several visits to Jordan during the autumn of 2002 to tie up details of basing rights for US commando units, helicopters and attack jets, including F-16s and A-10s.

Preparations were also made to deploy US Patriot anti-missile batteries to Jordanian bases to enhance the missile defences around Israel. British special forces and the Royal Air Force Harrier squadrons were closely involved in these efforts, and they began training to operate from Jordan during October 2002. US special forces and British Special Air Service (SAS) and advance teams then visited Jordan under the cover of 'exercises', some reports suggesting that they crossed into Iraq at this time to observe targets.

These preparations and subsequent deployment of troops to the Hashemite Kingdom had to be cloaked under intensive secrecy owing to widespread pro-Iraqi feeling among Jordan's population. King Abdullah was taking a major gamble by joining the US-led war and reversing the policy of this father, King Hussein, of being neutral in the conflicts between the US and Iraq.

The build-up of US, British and Australian troops gained momentum during January and February 2003, when Azraq Airbase in north-eastern Jordan was activated as Gen Harrell's forward headquarters. Eventually some 10,000 Western troops were to be based in Jordan, with Azraq as the main base for fighter and reconnaissance aircraft, along with special-forces helicopters. The US Army's 5th Special Forces Group provided the main assault force, backed by Ranger battalions. Britain's 22nd Special Air Service Regiment and its Australian counterpart also moved to Jordan, while the British Royal Marines 45 Commando was assigned to support the SAS.

The USAF dispatched Lockheed F-16 Fighting Falcons and Fairchild A-10 Warthog squadrons of the Air National Guard, supported by combat search and rescue (CSAR) units with Sikorsky HH-60 Rescue Hawk helicopters and Lockheed HC-130P tankers. They were grouped under the 410th Air Expeditionary Wing. Eight RAF BAe Harrier GR7 strike jets and two English Electric Canberra PR9 surveillance aircraft were also deployed to Azraq. Jordanian basing was particularly important for these units, since they were not reliant on air-to-air refuelling to hit targets in western Iraq, which considerably reduced the pressure on the thinly stretched USAF tanker fleet.

The US Army's 160th Special Operations Aviation Regiment (Airborne) (SOAR(A)) provided the bulk of the assault helicopters, with eighteen Sikorsky MH-60

Pave Hawks, seven Hughes MH-6 Little Birds and fourteen Boeing MH-47 Chinooks. Attached to the 160th Regiment were eight British Boeing Chinook HC2s of the RAF's 7 Squadron and six Westland Lynx AH7s of the Army Air Corps 657 Squadron. The Australian Army's 5th Aviation Regiment completed the force with three Boeing Chinook CH-47Ds.

As US, British and Australian troops moved into Jordan, a smaller-scale deployment was taking place to the south in Saudi Arabia under conditions of even greater secrecy. USAF tanker units are understood to have set up base at Tabuk in north-western Saudi Arabia. Sikorsky HH-60H Rescue Hawks of the US Navy's Helicopter Combat Support Squadron 5 set up a forward base at Ar'ar on the Kingdom's northern border with Iraq, to provide CSAR coverage to the south of Baghdad.

Combat operations against western Iraq began even before President Bush's ultimatum expired in the early hours of 20 March. Reconnaissance teams were inserted into western Iraq, while no-fly-zone air patrols had carried out several air strikes against key communications links and air-defence radar sites.

In the early hours of 20 March, Little Bird gunships mounted simultaneous raids against Iraqi border posts to open up corridors for special-forces ground convoys to push across the border. The first targets were the airfield complexes at H-2 and H-3, which were the centre of Iraqi defences in the west and the most likely storage site of any Scud missiles. Ground and helicopter-borne troops quickly overcame the defences, with strong air support from the Jordan-based F-16s, A-10s and Harriers. These two captured airfields were quickly converted into forward operating bases for US, British and Australian forces.

Over the next two weeks the special forces teams began steadily moving towards the Euphrates valley, with US Rangers capturing the H1 airfield in a daring night-time parachute drop from Lockheed MC-130 Combat Talons on 25 March. Apart from their small forward operating bases, which were being guarded by Royal Marines and US Rangers, the special-forces teams did not try to occupy ground but moved fast to keep the small Iraqi garrisons in the region off guard. Travellers on the road from Baghdad to the Jordanian border reported few signs of the Western troops, apart from occasional vehicle checkpoints, suggesting they moved largely at night, away from populated areas.

The main opposition to the special forces came from Iraqi commando units, who were attempting to keep the main roads to Jordan and Syria open to allow key members of the regime to travel abroad and potential-ly escape if Baghdad should fall. When the Iraqis tried to rally resistance to US forces at their headquarters prison in the dusty town of Ar Rutbah, special forces directed an air strike onto the building during the early morning of 30 March.

Australian officers have given one of the few insights into the work of their Special Air Service patrols, who were operating closely with their British and US counterparts, in long-range reconnaissance and 'direct action' against various targets 'deep inside Iraq'. 'Our SAS task force has had a number of contacts, some initiated by the enemy, some by us', said a senior Australian officer. 'In some cases Iraqi troops were killed, military positions and equipment destroyed. In one incident special forces medics stopped to render medical assistance to two wounded soldiers before moving on.'

By the third week of the war, US British and Australian special-forces teams were operating well beyond the Euphrates valley. A vehicle patrol of the British Special Boat Service was ambushed by Iraqi troops in the desert to the west of Mosul on 1 April. The troops managed to break contact and move to a rendezvous point to be recovered by RAF Chinook helicopters.

On 2 April 160th SOAR conducted its most audacious raid of the war against Tharthar Palace, north-west of Baghdad. Little Bird gunships shot up Iraqi anti-aircraft guns to allow MH-47s to drop Rangers into the palace complex.

In three weeks of war, the special-forces task forces had pushed from Jordan to deep into central Iraq and swept all before them. Their mission had been to deny the Baghdad regime the use of western Iraq as a launch-pad for missile attacks on Egypt. No missiles were fired at Israel, but to date no Scuds have been found in the western desert.

On the southern flank in Kuwait, USAF special-forces aviation units were deployed to support the activities of the highly secret Task Force 20 (TF 20), which included elements of Delta Force commando unit, US Navy SEALs and Central Intelligence Agency para-military teams. These included Lockheed AC-130U Spook gunships and Sikorsky MH-53Ms of the 16th Special Operations Wing based at Ali Al Salem in Kuwait.

TF-20 reported direct to Gen Franks at Central Command forward headquarters in Qatar and was only used for strategic missions, such as locating weapons of mass destruction and regime leadership targets. The first mission of Task Force 20 was the securing of Iraqi oil installations around Basrah to prevent their sabotage. As in the west, reconnaissance teams were inserted inside Iraq well before the start of the war. During one of these missions on 19 March, an MH-53M had to put down inside Iraq with mechanical problems, and it was later destroyed by a US air strike. The 20th Special Operations Squadron then led the assault on the oil facilities on the Al Faw peninsular during the early hours of 21 March.

Over the next two weeks TF-20 helicopters were used to shuttle special-forces teams deep into Iraq, and to help these efforts they began operating from the US forward operating base at Tallil in southern Iraq. The most high-profile mission was the airlifting of the recovery force to Nasiriyah civilian hospital on 1 April to secure the US Army prisoner of war, Private Jessica Lynch.

The AC-130s found themselves in great demand during the US Army and US Marine Corps sieges of southern Iraqi cities, where they proved their worth targeting buildings containing paramilitaries in highly populated urban areas.

Special-forces aviation units may not have provided the most high-profile contribution to the war, but their impact may have been out of all proportion to their size.

Weapons loaders attach a guided munition to an Alabama Air National Guard F-16 Fighting Falcon at Azraq Airbase in Jordan prior to a mission against targets in western Iraq.
(USAF/Staff Sgt Bennie J. Davis)

F-16 Fighting Falcons from the 410th Air Expeditionary Wing return to Azraq Airbase in Jordan after a night mission over Iraq.
(USAF/Airman 1st Class Lindsey M. Slocum)

An RAF man from No. 39 Squadron conducts a security patrol at Azraq Airbase n Jordan.

(USAF/Staff Sgt Bennie J. Davis III)

A USAF HH-60G Pave Hawk helicopter of the 301st Rescue Squadron on combat search and rescue alert at Ali Al Salem Airbase in Kuwait.

(USAF/Staff Sgt Shane A. Cuomo)

An HH-60G Pave Hawk helicopter flight engineer from the 301st Rescue Squadron prepares for a mission from Ali Al Salem Airbase in Kuwait. Pave Hawk mission equipment includes a retractable in-flight refuelling probe, internal auxiliary fuel tanks, two crew-served 7.62 mm machine-guns and an 8,000-pound (3,600 kg) capacity cargo hook.

(USAF/Staff Sgt Shane A. Cuomo)

Maintenance personnel from the 410th Air Expeditionary Wing modify an external gun mount system on an HH-60G Pave Hawk helicopter at Azraq Airbase in Jordan. (USAF/Airman 1st Class Lindsey M. Slocum)

One of two RAF English Electric Canberra PR9s, deployed to Azraq in Jordan to fly surveillance missions over western Iraq. They use datalinks to download imagery in real time to ground stations. (US DoD/JCC(D))

An HH-60G Pave Hawk helicopter flight engineer from the 301st Rescue Squadron prepares for a mission from Ali Al Salem Airbase in Kuwait.
(USAF/Staff Sgt Shane A. Cuomo)

A USAF HH-60G Pave Hawk helicopter of the 301st Rescue Squadron and an HC-130 of the 39th Rescue Squadron conduct an aerial refuelling on 6 April over southern Iraq during a combat search and rescue mission.
(USAF/Staff Sgt Shane A. Cuomo)

Mission art is pictured on an RAF English Electric Canberra PR9 of 39 Squadron deployed to Azraq in Jordan. (Tim Ripley)

Australian CH-470 Chinook helicopters seen through night vision glasses. (Australian DoD)

Three CH-47D Chinook helicopters from the Australian Army's 5th Aviation Regiment deployed to Azraq in Jordan to support the country's Special Air Service Regiment, which fought alongside their British and American counterparts in western Iraq.

(Australian DoD)

Royal Australian Air Force C-130H Hercules of No. 36 Squadron supported the deployment of US, British and Australian special forces into Jordan. (Australian DoD)

Two HH-60 Pave Hawk helicopters of the 66th Rescue Squadron are loaded into a C-17 Globemaster III for deployment to Jordan. (USAF/Senior Airman Jeremy Smith)

CHAPTER 8
Drive on Baghdad

A week into Operation Iraqi Freedom, the US-led invasion of Iraq seemed to be stalled. Heavy sand storms and surprise guerrilla resistance in southern Iraq combined to slow the advance on Baghdad.

For US Army and Marine Corps commanders fighting against the sand, high winds, Iraqis and supply problems, the need was to regain momentum and prevent the Baghdad government from building a coherent defensive line south of its capital.

Early in the morning of 24 March, the US Army's V Corps had launched its 11th Aviation Brigade into action on a night-time 'deep strike' raid to hit the Republican Guard's Medina mechanized division. Its Boeing AH-64D Longbow Apache attack helicopter flew into a hornet's nest of anti-aircraft fire. One of the 11th Brigade's Apaches was shot down, another crashed in a dust cloud on take-off and thirty-three were hit by heavy Iraqi anti-aircraft artillery fire in the attack. Only seven of the brigade's Apaches were ready for action a week later, although eleven were reported to be under repair. Two captured Apache crewmen were later paraded on Baghdad TV, although the Pentagon denied the $50 million helicopter had been shot down by an Iraqi farmer. Sand storms now engulfed the battlefield, and further attack helicopter strikes were not possible. Now was the time for US, British and Australian airmen to step up their game to help clear the way for the ground forces.

The commander of the US Third Army, Lt-Gen David McKiernan, and his senior US Air Force Advisor, Maj-Gen Dan Leaf, set their staffs to work to ramp up the level of air support for US troops fighting towards Baghdad.

On call was an impressive force of aircraft and helicopters, optimized for attacking enemy ground forces. The US Army's V Corps had more than 100 Boeing AH-64D Apache Longbow attack helicopters, assigned to the 3rd Infantry and 101st Airborne Divisions, as well as the 11th Aviation Brigade.

Supporting the US Marines Corps I Marine Expeditionary Force (I MEF) were the 400 aircraft and helicopters of the 3rd Marine Air Wing (MAW), including McDonnell Douglas AV-8B and F/A-18C/D Hornet strike jets and Bell AH-1W Super Cobra helicopter gunships.

USAF support included a force of four squadrons of Fairchild A-10A Warthog 'tank busters', backed up by several squadrons of Lockheed Martin F-16C Fighting Falcons and McDonnell Douglas F-15E Strike Eagles. Some twenty-eight Boeing B-52H Stratofortress and 11 Rockwell B-1B Lancer heavy bombers were also on call to aid the close-air-support effort with dumb bombs or satellite-guided Joint Direct Attack Munitions (JDAMs). Hornet and Grumman F-14 Tomcat strike aircraft on the three US Navy carriers in the Gulf were also primarily tasked to support the attack effort.

Allied contributions to this effort were British RAF Panavia Tornado GR4 and BAe Harrier GR7 aircraft and Royal Australian Air Force Hornets.

In total, more than 800 strike aircraft and attack helicopters were available to support General McKiernan's troops, and for the next week more than 600 attack sorties a day were flown. General Leaf's staff began generating a 'direct support air tasking order' to co-ordinate all these aircraft into a single integrated attack plan.

Even before US-led forces crossed the border into Iraq on 20 March, the Iraqi leader Saddam Hussein had deployed his defences in the south of Iraq. Holding the border with Kuwait, Basra and Nasiriyah was the job of three regular army divisions, backed up by Ba'ath Party militia troops and Saddam Fedayeen fighters. Although outnumbered and outgunned, for the first two weeks of the war these rag-tag troops caused the US and British forces major headaches after they launched a guerrilla campaign in southern Iraq.

To hold the southern approaches to Baghdad, Saddam Hussein posted six divisions of his supposedly élite Republican Guard Forces Command (RGFC). The first defensive line was set up along a line between the towns of Karbala and Al Kut, with the Median armoured division in the west, the Al Nida armoured division in the centre and the Baghdad mechanized division out to the east. Elements of the Nebuchadnezzar and Hammurabi mechanized divisions were deployed just south of Baghdad, as a second line of defence.

The task given to the US-led air forces was to render these units combat ineffective before the main elements of the ground forces were committed to action.

General Leaf and his direct boss, the USAF commander in the Middle East, Lt-Gen Michael 'Buzz' Moseley, turned to tried and tested tactics to do the job. Targets behind the front-line were the responsibility of air commanders to destroy, and a system of 'kill boxes' was set up over the main Iraqi troop positions. The location of targets within the 'kill boxes' was the job of fast jet 'forward air controllers - airborne' (FAC-A) who circled above them for hours at a time. Also known as Strike Co-ordinating Armed Reconnaissance (SCAR), these were usually two-seat Hornets, Strike Eagles and Tomcats. They required special qualifications and were much in demand to ensure constant coverage was maintained over the Iraqi battlefield to maintain the tempo of 'kill box' close air support, or Kick-CAS.

Iraqi troops in direct battle or 'contact' with US troops were dealt with by close air support, directed by forward air controllers riding in armoured vehicles with the tank spearheads. Air controllers in Boeing E-3 Sentry AWACS were responsible for the minute-by-minute massaging of these fire-control measures to ensure that maximum damage was inflicted on the Iraqis and that the risk of friendly fire was kept to the minimum.

Lt-Gen William Wallace, commander of V Corps, put his main effort into destroying the Medina division around Karbala. For a week up until 2 April, he pounded the Medina division with artillery and rocket launchers, while fixed aircraft joined in the battle, striking both close air support and kill box or interdiction targets around the clock. Apache gunships were also able to join the battle now that the sand storms had lifted.

The Iraqi deployment perplexed many US and British pilots who, night after night, flew over the battlefield looking at targets through their thermal imaging night vision systems. They reported seeing hundreds of 'cold' tanks and artillery pieces parked up in central Iraq. 'It looked like they had been abandoned', said one RAF Harrier pilot. 'Intelligence told us that the Republican Guards who wanted to fight had gone south to fight. The ones left behind didn't have much fight and just went home rather than sitting around to be blown up by us.'

Strike aircraft systematically worked over the kill boxes, using laser or GPS-guided munitions to destroy or 'plink' individual Iraqi vehicles. 'Each aircraft would fly into a kill box with four weapons and come out without any weapons', said an A-10 pilot. US and British pilots reported very little Iraqi troop movements under this relentless bombardment, so they had little need to employ 'area' weapons such as 'cluster' bombs or B-52 'carpet bombing'. 'We saw hardly any massing of Iraqi tanks so could rely almost totally on precision-guided munitions', said an RAF pilot.

As the interdiction effort gained momentum, strike pilots started to begin to run out of valid targets, as the only Iraqi tanks and artillery surviving were positioned close to civilian areas, making them off limits because of collateral damage constraints. An increasing number of aircraft started to return to base with their bombs unused, so they started to be given secondary fixed targets to strike, such as Iraqi military barracks and ammunition dumps. Some 234 of these targets were hit during the war.

Over to the east, I MEF was fighting a similar battle against the Baghdad division to the south of Al Kut. Its infantry regimental combat teams were fighting against dogged Iraqi resistance in Nasiriyah, Qat al Sakkar, Ash Shatrah and Ad Diwaniyah, and they required constant close air support from Marine Cobras and Harriers. Meanwhile, Marine Hornets and Harriers joined the effort to hit kill boxes around Al Kut as part of a deep-strike effort, co-ordinated with artillery fire.

In the early hours of 2 April, both V Corps and I MEF rolled forward to crush what was left of the Republican Guard. The 3rd Infantry bypassed Karbala and raced north towards the Euphrates, with Apache gunships flying top cover. A few Iraqi tanks tried to resist the advance, but the Medina division had ceased to exist as a fighting formation. Those Republican Guards who wanted to fight retreated into Karbala to make a last stand. The 3rd Infantry's own aviation brigade and the 11th Brigade flew extensive flank-protection operations during this advance. To avoid the problems encountered during the previous week, these missions were fully integrated with air force suppression of enemy air defence (SEAD) and artillery support.

It was a similar picture in the east, where the 1st Marine Division met negligible resistance from the Baghdad division, as they seized a crossing over the Tigris. Marine Hornets and Harriers then shifted their emphasis to hitting the Iraqi IV Corps around Amara, near the Iranian border, to prevent it striking into I MEF's flank as it drove north towards Baghdad. Using information from IAI/TRW RQ-2 Pioneer unmanned aerial vehicles, 3rd MAW aircraft hit the only Iraqi armoured column that tried to move to engage the 1st Marine troops, inflicting heavy casualties.

Two days later the US Army and US Marines were at the gates of Baghdad, with the 3rd Infantry in control of the city's airport and the 1st Marine pushing into the eastern suburbs. Task Force 20 special-forces troops were already operating inside Baghdad and were waiting at Baghdad International Airport for the 3rd Infantry.

At the same time as the drive on Baghdad was under way, US and British troops were mopping up towns along the Euphrates that had become centres of resistance. Najaf, Karbala and Hillah were all swept by troops of the 101st Airborne Division, who flew by helicopter to secure them. Shayka Mazhar airfield was also captured in a divisional-sized air assault operation.

Further south the 2nd Brigade of the 82nd Airborne was securing Al Samawah with the help of Lockheed AC-130 Spectre gunships, while British troops were sweeping into Basrah. US Marines of the 24th Marine Expeditionary Unit and British paratroopers of 16 Air Assault Brigade rolled up Iraqi troops around Al Amara in a series of helicopter-borne moves.

With Iraqi resistance apparently crumbling, Gen McKiernan now decided to push his troops forward into the heart of Baghdad to complete the 'psychological fracture' of Saddam Hussein's government. It was hoped that the sudden appearance of US tanks in the heart of Baghdad would bring the Iraqi government crashing down. This was a high-risk strategy. 'This was the time to take risks', said General Leaf. 'We lost an A-10. There was a need to be aggressive, to take risks.'

To provide the close air support for the advancing soldiers and marines, a huge 'CAS stack' was created over Baghdad, which contained scores of strike aircraft armed with every type of ordnance in the US and British inventory. Aircraft were cycled through the stack on a 24-hour basis, to allow forward air controllers on the ground to instantly call aircraft into action with the necessary ordnance. Gen Moseley moved his tanker orbits deep over Iraq so that the close-air-support aircraft had easy access to fuel and could remain on station for long periods. The world's media caught much of this action live, broadcasting dramatic imagery of A-10s blasting an Iraqi ministry with 30 mm cannon. The RAF debuted its so-called 'inert', or concrete, bombs during this period, allowing targets to be hit with reduced blast effects to minimize collateral damage.

Co-ordinated Iraqi resistance had all but collapsed, allowing the US Army engineers to clear debris from the runways and taxi-ways of Baghdad Airport unhindered by artillery fire. This allowed USAF Lockheed C-130 Hercules transports to fly in on 6 April. A battalion of the 101st Airborne Division was flown into the airport by Boeing CH-46D Chinooks and Sikorsky UH-60 Black Hawks to bolster its defence.

As the US troops and marines fought the remnants of the Iraqi army, intelligence emerged that Saddam Hussein might be meeting his two sons in a Baghdad restaurant. Within some 47 minutes a B-1B was diverted to hit the location with four JDAMs. Saddam and his two sons escaped and the body of a child was dug out of the ruins.

By the afternoon of Wednesday 9 April, US troops were in the centre of the Iraqi capital and the leaders of the Iraqi regime were nowhere to be seen. Sporadic fighting continued around the city, with US Army Apaches and US Marine Cobras seeing action to support ground troops in action. The final close-air-support mission in the city was flown the following day, when US Marines were sent to seize a mosque where Saddam Hussein was said to be hiding. When they met fierce resistance, an A-10 was called from the CAS Stack to bomb a position near the mosque.

The securing of Baghdad did not mean the end of the ground war. Over the next five days, units of I MEF raced north to seize Saddam Hussein's home town of Tikrit. The kill-box system remained in place as the Republican Guard Adnan mechanized division based around Tikrit was pounded relentlessly. Marine forward arming and refuelling teams were pushed forward with the spearhead units to ensure Cobra gunships were always on hand to provide close air support. Iraqi resistance did result in one F-15E being shot down on 7 April over Tikrit.

By late on the evening of 13 April, US Marine armoured vehicles were on the outskirts of Tikrit, and it appeared that the Adnan division had melted away. Organized resistance to the US military had ceased.

Air support for the ground forces was the top priority for US, British and Australian airmen from the second week of the war, making up just over 50 per cent of air sorties, compared to 9.8 per cent against regime leadership or 10.2 per cent against weapons of mass destruction and 14.2 per cent to maintain air supremacy. The remainder of sorties were flown in support of special forces In the west and north. Out of some 25,240 individual aim points for air-delivered munitions identified by air planners before the invasion, some 12,983 were land targets, but in the end 15,593 land-force targets were identified and attacked, representing 79 per cent of all targets attacked.

MAJ-GEN DAN LEAF
Commander Air Component Co-ordination Element (ACCE), Camp Doha, Kuwait

"I had a new position, [established] within component commands where high tempo combat operations [are envisaged]", he said. "I provided a direct link between Coalition Forces Air and Land Component Commanders (CFACC) and (CFLCC)."

At the heart of the integration of air power to support the land advance was a system of what were termed 'fire support co-ordination measures' said the General. These were tried and tested from many previous conflicts. The key one was the fire support co-ordination line, or FSCL. This crucially delineated when strike aircraft could attack ground targets under the direction of air or land commanders. Beyond the FSCL was 'air force territory', with pilots being able to attack targets at will as long as their rules of engagement were followed. Battlefield interdiction missions beyond the FSCL usually channelled aircraft towards engagement zones or 'kill boxes', set up over concentrations of enemy tanks. Up to the FSCL, CAS could only be conducted under the positive control of a forward air controller (FAC) working with the ground forces. The positioning of the FSCL was therefore crucial because it determined the focus of air strikes on the battlefield. Those involved in this process describe it as a very dynamic and fast moving process, with the FSCL being moved several times during a day and kill boxes being 'opened' and 'closed' on a minute-by-minute basis as ground troops neared them, artillery fired through them or attack helicopters needed to service targets.

LT-COL 'SKEETER' GUS KOHNTOPP
Mission Planning Cell Chief, 190th Fighter Squadron, Idaho Air National Guard
Ahmed Al Jaber Airbase, Kuwait

'The big thing here was the classic close air support (CAS) role. We rarely flew against planned targets. They would send us to support troops in contact with the enemy, to find tanks and artillery firing on our troops, then we would take them out.

Most stuff we did was deep strike against open kill boxes. When the land forces paused, we bombed the Republican Guard Medina division. It didn't move. They were dispersed at the start, we didn't see many tanks moving. The troops abandoned their equipment and left. There were no tank-on-tank engagements, requiring CAS support.

Urban CAS in Baghdad was the worse case scenario. Hardest thing was to minimize collateral damage and identify targets. Trying to find targets among buildings without seeing gunfire was very hard to do. We had four A-10 squadrons here at Ahmed Al Jaber - the 75th, 172nd, 190th, 303rd Fighter Squadrons - making this the biggest concentration of A-10s since the Gulf war.

We used Maverick, Mk 82, HE rocket, gun 30 mm and a few CBU-87. The flexibility of A-10 meant we were used for escort of helicopters and C-130s, armed reconnaissance, sanitizing areas under air-to-air refuelling orbits, searching for Seersucker missiles, combat search and rescue and air interdiction. We were jacks-of-all-trades.'

GP CAPT MIKE HARWOOD

Commander RAF Harrier Detachment, Ahmed Al Jaber Airbase, Kuwait

According to the group captain, air power destroyed the Iraqi Regular Army, Republican Guard and Special Republican Guard. 'Their combat effectiveness was reduced to almost zero', he said. 'Air power destroyed organized military resistance. We and the Americans were sending 1,000 aircraft a day into Iraq, every day for three weeks, it was a hell of an effort.'

'Harriers contributed a range of airpower effects', he said. 'Everything here was about creating an effect. We intended having intelligence-led airpower. We have not seen precision like this before, the days of dump bombs are over. We took out one tank with a single Maverick and Paveway bomb.'

The Iraqi battlefield was very fast moving, and RAF Harrier pilots rarely took off knowing what there were to attack. Harwood said they relied on in-flight target briefings from airborne controllers in E-3 AWACS aircraft or army forward air controllers. 'Decision-making took place in cockpit by the pilot. In a single-seat aircraft a pilot became a lawyer, accountant and media man. Tactical actions had strategic effect.'

Harwood says that the RAF is already turning its attention to future conflict and learning tactical lessons from the recent experience. 'In Iraq we didn't fight the way we fought in Kosovo. We will win next time as well, not sure what tactics we will use then. I have the mind of doom.'

LT-COL DANIEL WILLIAMS AND MAJ DAVID J. RUDE

AH-64D Longbow Apache pilots, CO and operations officer, 1st Battalion (Attack) 3rd Aviation Regiment, US Army

'We were not fighting tanks in this war. Apaches were not sent after division artillery groups or large mechanized or armoured formations. The enemy was not arrayed as such. As the enemy's situation template became urban-centric instead of Soviet doctrine-based, with a conventional force in the open desert, the mission focus of the 1st Battalion, 3rd Aviation Regiment, transformed from massed battalion, or phased attacks against armour and artillery, to continuous close-combat attacks in support of the division's main-effort brigade combat team.

Due to concentrated anti-aircraft and small-arms threats all over the Iraqi battlefield, the battalion's aircraft always fought in teams and we refrained from launching single Apaches in combat operations. The lead aircraft focused eyes and fires out to their point, while the wingman provided local security for the team. The battalion commander, operating from an AH-64D, also provided local security behind the attack helicopter company in contact [with the enemy].

The fast-paced operational tempo required the battalion to be continuously postured to launch an Apache company within a 30-minute window, from the start of the ground war through to the seizure of Saddam International Airport.

In combat, only three [of our aircraft] sustained minor ground fire damage. One was destroyed on take-off due to drown-out conditions. The battalion fired 12,850 rounds of 30 mm, 584 rockets, 117 K-model 'laser' Hellfire and 21 'radio frequency' Hellfire missiles.'

A B-1 Lancer assigned to the 405th Air Expeditionary Wing based in Oman flew missions to support US troops advancing into southern Iraq. (USAF/Staff Sgt Cherie A. Thurlby)

F-16CJs assigned to the 379th Air Expeditionary Wing weather a sandstorm at Al Udeid during the second week of the war. The storm engulfed most of the Arabian peninsula and severely inhibited air operations. (USAF/Master Sgt Terry L. Blevins)

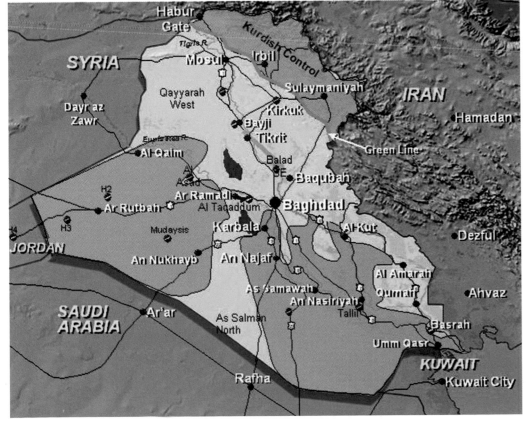

Two CH-46Es from HMM-268 taxi to refuel at Jalibah Airbase in southern Iraq before heading north to support the US Marine Corps advance on Baghdad.

(USMC/Sgt Nicholas S. Hizer)

This was the battle situation on 3 April 2003 as US troops closed in on Baghdad.

(US DoD Iraq Country Handbook)

A UH-60 Black Hawk helicopter of the US Army's 82nd Airborne Division lifts off for a medical evacuation mission during the advance on Baghdad. (USAF/Staff Sgt Shane A. Cuomo)

An F/A-18 Hornet from the USS Harry S. Truman flies a close-air-support mission over central Iraq. (US Navy/Cdr Thomas Lalor)

An A-10 Warthog aircraft rolls past an abandoned Iraqi tank at Tallil Airbase in southern Iraq, which was opened as a forward operating base for A-10 aircraft during the advance on Baghdad.
(USAF/2nd Lt Gerardo Gonzalez)

An A-10 Warthog pilot of the 75th Fighter Squadron surveys the battle damage to her aircraft after it had been hit over Baghdad during a close-air-support mission on 7 April. (USAF)

A US Army AH-64 Apache sets off for a night-time mission during the advance on Baghdad. (US Army)

Four squadrons of A-10A Warthog 'tankbuster' aircraft were based at Ahmed Al Jaber Airbase in Kuwait, which was the largest concentration of A-10s since the 1991 Gulf War. (Tim Ripley)

Ahmed Al Jaber Airbase in Kuwait was the hub of USAF and US Marine Corps close support efforts during the advance on Baghdad. (Tim Ripley)

An Iraqi Airways jet lies in ruins after the battle at Baghdad International Airport on 4 April.

(USMC/Sgt William Beezley)

Artwork on A-10A Warthog 'tankbusting' aircraft at Ahmed Al Jaber Airbase, Kuwait. (Tim Ripley)

B52 Stratofortress bombers armed with JDAM satellite-guided weapons provided close air support for US troops repeating tactics perfected in Afghanistan.
(US DoD/JCC(D))

Bomb artwork on Paveway laser-guided bomb on the wing of a F-16CG Fighting Falcon of the 524th Fighter Squadron at Ahmed Al Jaber Airbase, Kuwait. (Tim Ripley)

TO THE REPUBLICAN GUARD, HAPPY EASTER ASSHOLES!! FROM SEB & CASEY

US Marine Corps CH-53E Sea Stallions operated from shore bases or from the USS Kearsage, *which was cruising off the Kuwaiti coast.* (US DoD/JCC(D))

US Marine Corps AV-8B Harriers forward deployed to Ahmed Al Jaber Airbase in Kuwait, as well as operating from amphibious warfare ships off the coast of the emirate. (Tim Ripley)

RAF Harrier GR7s were operated from Ahmed Al Jaber Airbase in Kuwait, alongside their US Marine Corp AV-8B counterparts.

(Tim Ripley)

US Marine Corps F/A-18 Hornets and RAF Harrier GR7s prepare to launch for close-air-support missions from Ahmed Al Jaber Airbase in Kuwait.

(Tim Ripley)

A US Marine Corps AH-1A Cobra lands at a Forward Arming Refuelling Point in Tikrit, run by Marine Wing Support Squadron 373 during the final advance to capture the home town of Saddam Hussein. (USMC/Lance Cpl Nicholous Radloff)

111

Abandoned and destroyed military equipment, such as this T-55, littered the roads leading to Baghdad. (Staff Sgt Bryan P. Reed)

Saddam International Airport on the south western outskirts of Baghdad was a key objective for the US Army's 3rd Infantry Division. (US DoD/JCC(D)

Armament technicians prepare AIM-120 AMRAAM missiles for attachment to Royal Australian Air Force F/A-18 Hornets of No. 75 Squadron at Al Udeid Airbase. (Australian DoD)

Even aircraft-carriers in the Arabian Gulf, such as the USS Kitty Hawk, were affected by the sand storms that engulfed much of the Middle East during the second week of the war, severely hampering air operations. (US DoD/JCC(D))

The US Marine Corps opened up a series of captured Iraqi airfields, to allow its KC-130 Hercules transports to bring in supplies and to evacuate wounded. (US DoD/JCC(D))

CHAPTER 9

Northern Front

US war plans for the attack on Iraq had originally called for simultaneous assaults by air, sea and land from the north, west and south, with the aim of rapidly overwhelming Baghdad's defences.

While US Central Command was responsible for providing the forces attacking from Kuwait, Jordan, Saudi Arabia and other Gulf states, marshalling the forces for the northern front from Turkey was the job of US European Command. US and British aircraft were already based in Turkey to patrol the no-fly zone over Kurdish regions of Iraq, and it was envisaged that these forces would form the core of the northern front. Combined Task Force Northern Watch, based at Incirlik Airbase in southern Turkey, had evolved from the forces that had moved into Iraq in the spring of 1991 under the banner of Operation Provide Comfort to protect Kurds from Baghdad's troops. Up to March 2003 the force of some fifty fighter, strike, reconnaissance, tanker and rescue aircraft had mounted daily patrols over the Kurdish safe haven in northern Iraq, occasionally attracting anti-aircraft and surface-to-air missile (SAM) fire. The Iraqis, however, had generally kept out of the safe area, leaving the Kurds to run their own affairs under the leadership of the PUK and KDP groups.

Turkey had always been suspicious of the task force's operations because of an on-going rebellion by its own Kurdish minority. It regularly mounted raids into the safe area to destroy bases of the rebel PKK group. As a result, the Turks placed tight restrictions on US and British air patrols, and Turkish officers insisted on having joint command of them.

So when the US government began to approach the Turks in late 2002 to propose basing 60,000 troops for the northern front in their country, they received a far from positive response. The idea was for the 1st and 4th Infantry Divisions, supported by British armoured units, to attack into northern Iraq from Turkey, supported by more than 200 USAF strike aircraft based at Incirlik and other Turkish bases, or embarked on two US Navy aircraft-carriers. These aircraft were being provided by the main USAF units in Europe, including McDonnell Douglas F-15E Strike Eagles, Lockheed F-16 Fighting Falcons and Fairchild A-10 Warthogs. Special forces, reconnaissance and transport aircraft would support the Turkey-based air armada. A strong contingent of RAF aircraft, including SEPECAT Jaguar GR3 aircraft, was also supposed to support the northern front.

The diplomatic tension and confusion was increased when NATO plans to deploy Boeing E-3A Sentry AWACS and Dutch Raytheon Patriot missile defence batteries were vetoed by the French at Alliance headquarters in Brussels. Eventually this was resolved and the NATO defensive forces deployed to Turkey during late February.

The Turkish general staff backed the US plans, but the newly elected government was lukewarm and insisted the Ankara parliament vote on the issue. Turkish public opinion was overwhelmingly opposed to the US plans despite the offer of some $30 billion in loan guarantees and a further $6 billion in direct aid. This waving of financial aid failed to win over the Turks and its parliament voted down the proposal on 1 March.

In anticipation of a positive vote, the US military had already begun making preparatory moves for its deployment, and American logistic troops were already on ground in Turkey opening ports and setting up forward airbases. Advance elements of the USAF 352nd

Special Operations Group had set up a forward staging area at Constanta in Romania, along with 37th Airlift Squadron Lockheed C-130E Hercules tactical airlifters. McDonnell Douglas KC-10A Extender tankers had arrived at Bourgas in Bulgaria to support missions by thirteen Boeing B-52 Stratofortresses that had just arrived at RAF Fairford in the UK. Further Boeing KC-135 Stratotankers mustered at RAF Mildenhall to support the British-based B-52 force. A force of some 30 Boeing C-17 Globemaster airlifters also deployed to Rhein-Main in Germany, ready to support the movement of troops into northern Iraq.

The US Navy had also begun moving two carriers, the USS *Theodore Roosevelt* and USS *Harry S. Truman*, into the eastern Mediterranean, and to support their missions to Iraq the RAF opened its base at Akrotiri on Cyprus to USAF KC-135s and other support aircraft. The Greeks also opened Souda Bay on Crete for use by USAF tankers and reconnaissance aircraft.

Despite the Turkish parliament's decision, the US government still hoped to at least get Ankara to open its airspace and airbases to US aircraft so they could support the special-forces troops operating with Kurdish rebels in northern Iraq. Negotiations soon bogged down, and as the first US attack on Baghdad began in the early morning of 20 March, no agreement had yet been reached. This meant the air groups of the *Truman* and *Roosevelt* had to be diverted southwards over Egypt and Saudi Arabia to participate in the 'shock and awe' strikes on Baghdad. These strikes were organized at short notice, and the two carriers had to be moved south close to the Egyptian coast. Uncertainty about overflight rights also led the US Navy to move eight warships and five nuclear attack submarines from the Mediterranean into the Red Sea in the week before the outbreak of the war, to enable them to fire Raytheon BGM-109 Tomahawk Land Attack Missiles (TLAM) over Saudi Arabia into Iraq.

Late on 20 March, the Turkish parliament at last agreed to overflight rights, but it banned any aircraft participating in the raids from using Turkish airfields. This limitation meant US air commanders had to put in train a major reorganization of their plans to operate without the USAF and British aircraft at Incirlik. The *Truman* and *Roosevelt* were called back to the Turkish coast in preparation for launching sorties into northern Iraq. Special-forces Sikorsky MH-53M Pave Lows and Lockheed MC-130P Combat Shadow tankers were forward deployed to RAF Akrotiri on Cyprus ready to move ground troops into northern Iraq.

To help ease the diplomatic tensions with the Turks concerning overflight rights, the USAF now dispatched

Lt-Gen Glen W. Moorhead, the peacetime commander of the 16th Air Force at Aviano Airbase in Italy, to head a special team of 180 staff officers at Incirlik, dubbed Coalition Air Forces North.

By 24 March, the air offensive on the northern front opened in earnest, with strike packages being launched around the clock from the *Truman* and *Roosevelt*. US forward air-controller teams from the 10th Special Forces Group working with the Kurds began to step up the pressure on 150,000 Iraq troops around Mosul and Kirkuk. If the US could not take the offensive on the ground, then it was hoped to use airpower to keep them pinned down and prevent them moving south to join the defence of Baghdad.

Although Kurds had prepared airstrips on their territory for use by fixed-wing aircraft for the first days of the war, the MH-53Ms and MC-130s of the 352nd Group were the main way of moving troops and supplies to the special-forces teams in northern Iraq. The wing aircraft and helicopters flew some 4,300 personnel and 375 million pounds of cargo into two forward operating locations in Kurdistan.

This situation changed on 26 March when 1,000 US Army paratroopers of the 173rd Airborne Brigade mounted a combat parachute drop to secure Bashur airstrip in northern Iraq. A fleet of C-17s launched from Aviano Airbase in Italy carrying the paratroopers, protected by three waves of attack aircraft launched from the two US Navy carriers in the Mediterranean. They attacked Iraqi headquarters and artillery positions within range of Bashur. In the event, the US airborne landing was unopposed, and within hours technicians from the USAF 86th Contingency Response Group began preparing the airstrip to receive further follow-up flights of C-17s and C-130s.

For almost three weeks of continuous operations, the *Truman*'s and *Roosevelt*'s air wing kept up a round-the-clock air presence over northern Iraq. The *Truman* flew mainly day operations and *Roosevelt* concentrated on night missions. The 400-mile flight from the eastern Mediterranean meant US Navy fliers often spent between five and six hours in their cockpits during these missions. TLAMs could also now be used to hit targets in northern Iraq and were used on 28 March to blast at the mountain base of the Ansar al-Islam group before Kurdish peshmerga fighters, backed by American special-forces troops, stormed the base.

This 'long-distance' war had many similarities with the Afghanistan campaign of 2001. On the ground small special-forces teams were working hand in glove with Kurdish rebels and were applying precise aerial firepower carried by US Navy aircraft to break the morale of Iraqi defenders. B-52s from RAF Fairford joined this effort on a daily basis, and their large bomb loads resulted in Iraqi positions being saturated with Joint Direct Attack Munitions (JDAMs). As in Afghanistan, the B-52s were able to orbit over Iraqi positions for several hours at a time, waiting to be directed by special-forces teams to drop individual bombs against pin-point targets, or putting in 'area' attacks against larger targets. The Fairford B-52s also debuted the Rafael/Northrop Grumman Litening 2 laser-designating pod to direct laser-guided bombs against a target on the northern front.

Iraqi resistance to this aerial onslaught was furious at first, and some eighty Raytheon AGM-88 HARM anti-radar missiles were fired against air-defence sites in northern Iraq.

As US troops surged into Baghdad during the first week of April, the northern front was also beginning to unravel. To boost its ground forces, the US Army flew M1A1 Abrams tanks of the 1st Infantry Division into Bashur from Germany. The US Marine Corps 26th Marine Expeditionary Unit also overflew Turkey in its Sikorsky CH-53E Sea Stallions and Boeing Vertol CH-46E Sea Knight helicopters from the USS *Iwo Jima* to join the battle in northern Iraq.

By 10 April Kurdish forces were surging forward and had taken Kirkuk. The following day Iraqi commanders in Mosul surrendered and their troops started deserting en masse. From the south, US Marines of Task Force Tripoli were racing north from Baghdad to capture Tikrit, Saddam Hussein's birthplace. The task force of three Light Armoured Reconnaissance battalions received massive air support from both the north and the south, so there was little organized resistance when it entered Tikrit on 13 April. Some 800 close-air-support sorties were tasked against targets around Tikrit, and 200 munitions were dropped. By this point *Truman*'s air wing along had flown 1,946 sorties and dropped 1,198 munitions, of which more than 90 per cent were precision-guided weapons. The *Roosevelt*'s aircraft flew to a similar level of intensity, while RAF Fairford's B-52s flew 120 missions and dropped 2,700 munitions.

In the course of almost three weeks of sustained aerial bombardment, the back of Iraq's northern defences had been broken. The combination of special forces on the ground, US Navy strike forces and USAF shore-based support assets had proved effective and turned General Franks's concept of a northern front into a deadly reality.

PERSONNEL E-MAIL FROM COL CHARLIE CLEVELAND

Commander Joint Special Operations Task Force - North to Captain Mark 'Cyprus' Vance, Commander Carrier Air Wing 3 embarked on the USS *Harry S. Truman*.

On behalf of the Special Forces A teams and the rest of us here at Task Force Viking, I want to say thanks for being there when we needed you. You were instrumental in our dismantling three [Iraqi army] corps and the ultimate capture of the third and fourth largest cities in Iraq. Says a lot considering the ground component largely consisted of the 10th Special Forces Group (Airborne) and our Kurdish allies. We took some big risks knowing that when needed, you'd be there. You never failed us and as a direct result, we never lost a position and only had four casualties during the entire operation. Please pass to your aircrews and their ship mates our congratulations and thanks for a job well done. Don't know when or where, but I'm sure our paths will cross again. When they do, I'll buy the beer.

[Quoted in *The Hook*, Journal of Carrier Aviation, Summer 2003 edition.]

The US Navy Support Activity at Souda Bay on Crete quickly became home to USAF tanker, electronic-warfare and intelligence-gathering aircraft. The Greek government did not publicly acknowledge that the base was being used to support the war against Iraq. (US DoD/JCC(D))

Incirlik Airbase in Turkey was the home to USAF and other aircraft patrolling the northern no-fly zone from April 1991 to March 2003. F-16 Fighting Falcons and KC-135 Stratotankers were the core of the force operating from Turkey. (USAF)/JCC(D))

Aviano Airbase in Italy was used as the launch pad for the parachute drop by the US Army's 173rd Airborne Brigade into northern Iraq on 26 March. (US DoD/JCC(D))

An SA-332 Super Puma chartered from Geo-Seis Helicopters is given the signal to lift off from the flight deck of USS Harry S. Truman. The helicopters provided logistic support for 6th Fleet ships in the eastern Mediterranean. (US Navy/Photographer's Mate Airman Ryan O'Connor)

JDAMs are loaded onto one of four aircraft elevators for transport to the ship's flight deck aboard USS Harry S. Truman for loading onto Iraq-bound strike jets. (US Navy/Photographer's Mate 3rd Class Danny Ewing)

F-14 Tomcats prepare to catapult from the USS Harry S. Truman on the first night of the war, when aircraft from the carrier attacked targets in western Iraq. (US Navy/Photographer's Mate 1st Class Michael W. Pendergrass)

An F/A-18 Hornet is prepared for launch from the USS Harry S. Truman as strikes against northern Iraq gather momentum. (US Navy/Photographer's Mate 3rd Class Danny Ewing)

An EC-130H Compass Call with the 398th Air Expeditionary Group takes off from Souda Bay on Crete for a mission to jam Iraqi communications. (USAF/Tech Sgt Robert J. Horstman)

US Navy EP-3C Aries II aircraft were part of the 398th Air Expeditionary Group based at Souda Bay on Crete to monitor Iraqi communications and radar activity. (USAF/Tech Sgt Robert J. Horstman)

An F/A-18 Hornet VMFA-115 refuels from a USAF KC-135 Stratotanker during a mission over northern Iraq. Without support from USAF tankers, the US Navy fighters based on carriers in the eastern Mediterranean would not have been able to reach targets in Iraq. (US Navy)

KC-135 Stratotankers assigned to the 401st Air Expeditionary Wing sit ready on the flight line at RAF Akrotiri on Cyprus. Almost thirty KC-135s were based on the island, which had a key strategic position in the eastern Mediteranean. (USAF/Master Sgt Mark Bucher)

After dropping off pallets of food and equipment, a C-130 Hercules of the 37th Airlift Squadron takes off from Bashur Airfield in northern Iraq for its return flight to Romania. (USAF/Master Sgt Keith Reed)

121

An S-3B Viking of VS-22 refuels an F/A-18 Hornet of VFA-105 during a mission over northern Iraq. The small Vikings augmented the USAF KC-135s. (US Navy/Cdr Thomas Lalor)

An F/A-18 Hornet of VFA-37 heads towards targets in northern Iraq, armed with laser-guided bombs. (US Navy/Paul Farley)

An aerial gunner on an MH-53M Pave Low IV helicopter from the 21st Special Operations Squadron scans northern Iraq as the helicopter approaches Bashur Airfield. (USAF/Staff Sgt Jerry Morrison)

122

Aviano Airbase in Italy was used as the launch pad for the parachute drop by the US Army's 173rd Airborne Brigade into northern Iraq on 26 March.
(USAF/ Tech Sgt Stephen Faulisi)

Post-strike bomb damage assessment imagery of an Iraqi ballistic missile factory near Mosul.
(US DoD)

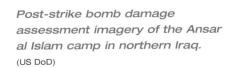

Post-strike bomb damage assessment imagery of the Ansar al Islam camp in northern Iraq.
(US DoD)

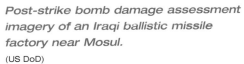

DESTROYED
SEVERE DAMAGE
LIGHT DAMAGE

JS141551

Aircrew of the 398th Air Expeditionary Group prepare an RC-135 Rivet Joint aircraft for a mission from Souda Bay on Crete to monitor Iraqi communications and radar activity.
(USAF/Tech Sgt Robert J. Horstman)

An MH-53M Pave Low IV helicopter from the 21st Special Operations Squadron on a mission into northern Iraq to support US special forces troops working with Kurdish rebel groups. (US DoD/JCC(D))

A B-52 Stratofortress from the 457th Air Expeditionary Group takes off for its 100th combat mission from RAF Fairford on 11 April. Aircrews from the British base flew more than 1,200 hours and dropped more than 2,400 bombs during the war.
(US DoD/JCC(D))

CHAPTER 10

Occupation

When US President George Bush declared on 1 May 2003 that major combat operations in Iraq had ended, it did not mean that the US-led air activity also ceased.

US Central Command quickly authorized a drawdown in the fixed-wing strike aircraft and specialist support aircraft that had been at the forefront of the air campaign against Baghdad. However, the decision by the US and British governments to occupy Iraqi with a 150,000-strong garrison of troops meant there was a need for continued air support, though in a very different form.

The attack helicopters of the main US Army and US Marine Corps divisions took on the brunt of responsibility for close air support for troops carrying out internal security and humanitarian aid operations in Iraq.

USAF participation in the occupation effort was extensive and centred on four large former Iraqi airbases, which were being converted into forward operating bases. Baghdad International Airport became the main transport hub for US military traffic supporting the garrison in the capital and the Coalition Provisional Authority. Tallil in the south, Kirkuk in the north and H-1 in the west were transformed into forward operating bases, complete with detachments of USAF Fairchild A-10A Warthog close-air-support aircraft and General Atomic RQ-1 Predator and Sikorsky HH-60 Pave Hawk helicopters.

Further afield in the Middle East, operations were wound down at Prince Sultan Airbase (PSAB) in Saudi Arabia and at many of the other bases in the region. Al Udeid Airbase in Qatar became the new home of the Combined Air Operations Centre (CAOC), as well as units of Lockheed F-16 Fighter Falcon fighters

McDonnell Douglas F-15E Strike Eagles. Ahmed Al Jaber Airbase in Kuwait emptied of the hundreds of USAF, RAF and US Marine Corps fighters that had supported the advance on Baghdad, but the RAF retained a small detachment of BAE Systems GR4 Tornadoes at Ali Al Salem Airbase in the Emirate to support the British division in Basra. From having several hundred fast jets and bombers available at the start of the war, US and British air commanders now required only a few score fast jets. The US Navy continued to maintain a carrier strike group in Middle East waters.

Logistic support for the US troops was a top priority, and the USAF fleet of Boeing C-17 Globemasters and Lockheed C-130 Hercules found itself heavily tasked.

As attacks on US occupation forces, now dubbed Combined Joint Task Force 7, started to escalate during May and into June, the US command in Baghdad was preparing a series of 'cordon and search' operations to catch members of the guerrilla groups responsible. The first, Peninsula Strike, was aimed at the Fallujah region at the centre of the so-called 'Sunni Triangle', north-west of Baghdad. It was followed by Operations Desert Scorpion, Sidewinder, Soda Mountain and Ivy Serpent. These involved air assault operations into remote areas at night by infantry units of the 101st Airborne and 4th Infantry Divisions.

Resistance to these operations was mixed, and the heaviest opposition was met in June by the 101st Airborne, when it raided what was described as an 'insurgent camp' in north-west Baghdad. One of the supporting Apaches was shot down by hostile fire but the crew were rescued. C-130 transport approaching Baghdad Airport were also attacked on several occasions by shoulder-launched heat-seeking missiles, but no hits were recorded.

The most-high-profile air operations involved those in

support of Task Force 20 as it hunted down leaders of Iraq's former government. One attack that did not go according to plan was when task force special forces troops, hunting Iraqi leaders, called in a Predator to attack a convoy with Hellfire missiles. Unfortunately the convoy was in neutral Syria and was not hostile.

The special forces teams had better luck on 22 July when they joined troops of 101st Airborne Division to sur-

round a house in Mosul, where Saddam Hussein's sons Uday and Qusay were hiding. In a heavy firefight that involved Bell OH-58D Kiowa Warriors firing 2.75-inch rockets, the occupants of the house were killed. Saddam Hussein remained at large until December when he was captured by US troops near his home town of Tikrit.

An F-117 of the 8th Fighter Squadron returns home to Holloman AFB on 18 April as part of the rapid draw-down in US airpower in the Middle East.
(US DoD/JCC(D))

Pararescuemen from the 304th Rescue Squadron are hoisted up to an HH-60G Pave Hawk at Tallil Airbase, Iraq, during a training mission after the war. The base was built up as the main USAF 'hub' in southern Iraq.
(USAF/Staff Sgt Shane A. Cuomo)

USAF experts collect data from a Coalition precision-guided munition strike through the roof of the Ba'ath Party headquarters building during Operation Iraqi Freedom. They were part of the 100-strong group of the Combined Weapons Effectiveness Assessment Team that visited some 500 sites to assess how well US weapons achieved their intended effects during Operation Iraqi Freedom. (USAF/Capt Patricia Lang)

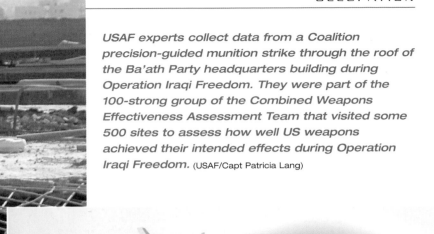

Technicians from the 64th Expeditionary Reconnaissance Squadron prepare a Predator unmanned aerial vehicle for a mission. Predators are assigned to support Task Force 20's hunt for former leaders of the Iraqi government.

(USAF/Master Sgt Deb Smith)

An RAF C-130J Hercules transport fires flares during its final approach to Baghdad International Airport to decoy away shoulder-launched heat-seeking missiles fired by Iraqis opposed to the US-led occupation. Several aircraft have been fired upon in the vicinity of the airport. (USAF/Master Sgt Robert R. Hargreaves Jr)

USAF experts use heavy equipment to pull a MiG-25R Foxbat-B from beneath the sands at Al-Taqqadum Airfield west of Baghdad, where a US military search team has uncovered several MiG-25s and Su-25 ground-attack jets found buried. (USAF/Master Sgt T. Collins)

The USAF's fleet of C-5 Galaxy strategic transport aircraft were heavily used to airlift cargo needed by the occupation forces into newly opened airfields inside Iraq. (US DoD/JCC(D))

Pararescuemen on board an HH-60G Pave Hawk of the 304th Rescue Squadron. (USAF/Staff Sgt Shane A. Cuomo) (US DoD/JCC(D))

The 101st Airborne Division mounted regular air assault operations in northern Iraq, using its fleet of UH-60 Black Hawks to move troops to search for Iraqi guerrilla fighters opposing the US-led occupation. (US DoD/JCC(D))

USAF A-10A Warthog jets taxi out for a mission from Tallil Airbase. (US DoD/JCC(D))

US Army UH-60 Black Hawk crewmen await a mission at a forward base inside Iraq. (US DoD/JCC(D))

MUNITIONS USED IN IRAQ
Munition Expenditure During the Iraq War

USAF, USMC and US NAVY

Raytheon GBU-10 Paveway laser-guided bombs	236
Raytheon GBU-12 Paveway laser-guided bombs	7,114
Raytheon GBU-16 Paveway laser-guided bombs	1,223
Raytheon GBU-24 Paveway laser-guided bombs	23
Raytheon GBU-27 Paveway laser-guided bombs	11
Raytheon GBU-28 Paveway laser-guided bombs	1
Boeing GBU-31 JDAMs satellite-guided bombs	5,086
Boeing GBU-32 JDAMs satellite-guided bombs	768
Boeing GBU-35 JDAMs satellite-guided bombs	675
Boeing GBU-37 JDAMs satellite-guided bombs	13
Raytheon BGM-109 Tomahawk Land Attack Missiles (TLAM)	802
Boeing AGM-130 stand-off missiles	4
Raytheon AGM-154 (JSOW) Joint Stand-Off Weapons	253
Boeing AGM-86C/D (CALCM) Conventional Air-Launched Cruise Missiles	153
Raytheon EGBU-27 GPS/laser-guided bombs	98
Lockheed Martin AGM-114 Hellfire missiles	802
AGM-84 Raytheon (SLAM (ER)) Stand-off Land Attack Missiles	3
Raytheon AGM-88 (HARM) High Speed Anti-Radiation Missiles	408
Lockheed Martin CBU-103 Wind-Corrected Munitions	818
Total Guided Munitions	**19,948**

M117 750 lb iron' bombs	1,625
Mk-82 500 lb iron' bombs	5,505
Mk-83 1,000 lb 'iron' bombs	1,693
Mk 84 2,000 lb 'iron' bombs	6
CBU-87 cluster bombs	118
Rockeye Mk 99 cluster bombs	182
Mk 77 fire bombs/napalm	?
Total Unguided Munitions	**9,251**

Rounds of 20 mm ammunition	16,901
Rounds of 30 mm ammunition	311,597
PDU-5 and M129 leaflet dispenser bombs	348

RAF

Raytheon Enhanced Paveway II GPS/laser-guided bombs	394
Raytheon Enhanced Paveway III GPS/laser-guided bombs	10
Raytheon II Paveway laser-guided bombs	265
Raytheon AGM-65 Maverick missiles	38
MBDA Storm Shadow cruise missiles	27
BAe Dynamics ALARMs	47
Hunting RBL-755 cluster bombs	66
1,000 lb 'iron bombs'	72

An air-launched cruise missile goes into the belly of a B-52 Stratofortress on 20 March.
(USAF/Senior Airman Christina M. Rumsey)

Aviation Ordnance personnel from Carrier Air Wing Eight (CVW-8) and USS Theodore Roosevelt *(CVN 71) discuss the distribution of ordnance on the ship's flight deck.*
(US Navy/Photographer's Mate Airman Recruit Chris Thamann)

Bomb loaders from the 335th Expeditionary Fighter Squadron prepare to mount an AGM-130 on an F-15E Strike Eagle at Al Udeid Airbase, Qatar. (USAF/Staff Sgt Derrick C. Goode)

Concrete or 'inert' GPS-guided Enhanced Paveway bombs at Ahmed Al Jaber Airbase, Kuwait.

(Tim Ripley)

GPS-guided Enhanced Paveway bombs on RAF Tornado GR4s at Ali Al Salem Airbase, Kuwait.

(Tim Ripley)

A Northrop Grumman Litening pod on an AV-8B Harrier Jump Jet of the 3rd US Marine Corps Air Wing at Ahmed Al Jaber Air base, Kuwait.

(Tim Ripley)

A JDAM GPS satellite-guided bomb on a Lockheed Martin F-16CG Fighting Falcon of the 524th Fighter Squadron at Ahmed Al Jaber Airbase, Kuwait. (Tim Ripley)

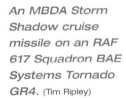

Weapons on A-10s at Ahmed Al Jaber Airbase, Kuwait, are, from left to right, a Raytheon AGM-65 Maverick missile, 2.75 in rockets and Jamming pod.

(Tim Ripley)

An MBDA Storm Shadow cruise missile on an RAF 617 Squadron BAE Systems Tornado GR4. (Tim Ripley)

A TIALD pod on an RAF Tornado as it is prepared for no-fly-zone patrols at Ali Al Salem Airbase in Kuwait.

(Tim Ripley)

133

An RAF Tornado GR4 at Ali Al Salem Airbase, Kuwait, with a RAPTOR reconnaissance pod.
(Tim Ripley)

USAF crewmen check a Paveway laser-guided bomb inside the weapon bay of a B-52 Stratofortress at RAF Fairford prior to a mission over northern Iraq. The bombs were used in conjunction with Litening pods.

A Vinten Joint Reconnaissance Pod on an RAF Harrier GR7 at Ahmed Al Jaber Airbase, Kuwait.
(Tim Ripley)

US AND UK AIRCRAFT LOSSES DURING IRAQI OPERATIONS, FEBRUARY–JUNE 2003

Date	Location	Type	Unit	Serial	Casualties	Cause	Level damage/Result
25 Feb	Kuwait	UH-60	US Army 5/158th Avn Regt		4 killed	accident during night exercise	
19 Mar	southern Iraq	MH-53M	USAF 16th SOW		1 injured	accident	air strike destroyed wreckage
20 Mar	northern Kuwait/Iraq?	AH-64	US Army		Nil	sand storm/mechanical?	
21 Mar	Kuwait	CH-46E	USMC HMM-268		12 dead	sand storm/mechanical?	total loss
22 Mar	northern Arabian Gulf	Sea King AEW Mk 7	RN A Flight 849 NAS	XV650 'CU-182'	7 dead total	air-to-air collision caused by weather?	total loss
22 Mar	northern Arabian Gulf	Sea King AEW Mk 7	RN A Flight 849 NAS	XV704 'R-186'	7 dead total	air-to-air collision caused by weather?	total loss
23 Mar	north Ali Al Salem, Kuwait	Tornado GR4	RAF 9 Squadron	ZG710 'D'	2 dead	US PAC-2 Patriot	total loss
24 Mar	near Karbala	AH-64D	US Army C Coy, 1-227th Avn Regt	99-5135	2 POW	Iraqi fire/mechanical?	captured intact by Iraqis
24 Mar	near Karbala	AH-64D	US Army 11th Aviation Brigade	00-5232	nil	Iraqi fire/mechanical?	part of 11th Aviation Brigade attack 11 AH-64D repaired in 4 days
24 Mar	central Iraq	CH-47D	US Army 159th Aviation Regt		nil	Iraqi fire	light damage continued mission, flying with above
24 Mar	central Iraq	CH-47D	US Army 159th Aviation Regt		nil	Iraqi fire	light damage continued mission, flying with above
25 Mar	southern Iraq	u/l helicopter	USMC		3 injured	sand storm	

Date	Location	Type	Unit	Serial	Casualties	Cause	Level damage/ Result
25 Mar	southern Iraq	u/l helicopter	USMC		3 injured	Wire strike during CAS mission	total loss
25 Mar	Basrah	Phoenix UAV	British Army 32 Regt RA	ZJ300		Landing accident	total loss
25 Mar	southern Iraq	AH-64D	US Army, 1-3rd Avn Regt		nil	Landing accident	
25 Mar	near Baghdad	RQ-1K Predator	USAF 57th Wing			Iraqi fire	Landed successfully
25 Mar	southern Iraq	UH-60	US Army, 2-3rd Regt		nil	sand storm	total loss
? Mar	central Iraq	Hunter	US Army V Corps		nil	Iraqi AAA	aircraft repaired
? Mar	central Iraq	Hunter	US Army V Corps		nil	accident	total loss
? Mar	central Iraq	Hunter	US Army V Corps		nil	Iraqi SAM	total loss
? Mar	central Iraq	Pioneer	USMC VMU-1		nil	Iraqi SAM	repaired
26 Mar	southern Iraq	UH-1N	USMC		nil	Iraqi SAM	repaired
pre 26 Mar	Basrah	Phoenix UAV	British Army 32 Regt RA	ZJ393		Iraqi fire/ mechanical?	total loss
27 Mar	central Iraq	RQ-1K Predator	USAF 57th Wing 11th RS	95-3014 'WA'		Iraqi fire/ mechanical?	total loss
28 Mar	Baghdad	RQ-1K Predator	USAF 57th Wing			Iraqi fire/ mechanical?	total loss
28 Mar	FOB Shell, near Najaf	AH-64D	US Army B Coy 2-101st Aviation Regt	98-5068	2 injured	sand storm	total loss
28 Mar	FOB Shell, near Najaf	AH-64D	US Army A Coy 2-101st Aviation Regt	97-5032	2 injured	sand storm hit power cables	total loss
28 Mar	FOB Shell, near Najaf	OH-58D(I)	US Army 2-101st Aviation Regt		2 injured	sand storm	damaged in landing

Date	Location	Type	Unit	Serial	Casualties	Cause	Level damage/ Result
28 Mar	FOB Shell, near Najaf	OH-58D(I)	US Army 2-101st Aviation Regt		2 injured	sand storm	damaged in landing
28 Mar	Iraq	OH-58D	US Army A Troop 2-17th Cavalry	95-0024		accident	total loss
28 Mar	Iraq	OH-58D	US Army A Troop 2-17th Cavalry	9			badly damaged
28 Mar	Basrah	Phoenix UAV	British Army 32 Regt RA	ZJ417		Iraqi fire/ mechanical?	badly damaged
30 Mar	RAF Akrotiri, Cyprus	KC-135R	USAF 351st ARS	63-8025	nil	accident, nose wheel collapsed	repaired on site
30 Mar	southern Iraq	UH-1N	USMC HMLA-169	160620 SN-39	3 killed, 1 injured	Iraqi fire	total loss
30 Mar	near Hillah	AH-64D	US Army 2-101st Aviation Regt		1 injured	accident	aircraft lost
30 Mar	near Hillah	AH-64D	US Army 2-101st Aviation Regt		nil	accident	repaired
30 Mar	Ali AL Salem AB, Kuwait	CH-53E	USMC	23'	nil	landing accident	very serious damage
31 Mar	near Najaf	AH-64D	US Army 1-3rd Aviation Regiment	99-5104	1 injured	Iraqi fire	repaired
31 Mar	central Iraq	AH-64D	US Army 3-101st Aviation Regt		nil	landing accident	?
?? Mar	near Karbala	UH-60L	US Army 159th Aviation Regt				total loss
?? Apr	Basrah	Phoenix UAV	British Army 32 Regt RA	ZJ411		Iraqi fire/ mechanical?	total loss
?? Mar	near Karbala	UH-60L	US Army 159th Aviation Regt				total loss

Date	Location	Type	Unit	Serial	Casualties	Cause	Level damage/ Result
01 Apr	northern Arabian Gulf	S-3B	US Navy VS-38		2 injured	landing accident on USS *Constellation*	total loss
01 Apr	northern Arabian Gulf	AV-8B	USMC HMM-263		1 injured	landing accident on USS *Nassau*	total loss
02 Apr	southern Iraq	F-14A	US Navy VF-154		1 injured	mechanical problem	total loss
02 Apr	near Karbala	UH-60A	US Army B Coy 2-3rd Aviation Regt		6 killed	accident	total loss
03 Apr	south of Baghdad	F/A-18C	US Navy VFA-195	164974 NF-405	1 killed	US PAC-3 Patriot?	total loss
03 Apr	Iraq	AH-64D	US Army B Coy 2-101st Aviation Regt	97-5035		Iraqi fire	light damage
04 Apr	Basrah	Phoenix UAV	British Army 32 Regt RA	ZJ402		rolled of runway	repaired
05 Apr	Ali Azzizayal, central Iraq	AH-1W	USMC HMLA-267	161020	2 killed	sand storm	total loss
06 Apr	Kuwait	UH-60A	US Army 571st Med Coy	87-24624	? injured	landing accident	total loss
06 Apr	central Iraq	UH-60L	US Army B Coy 4-101st Aviation Regt	93-26522	? injured	landing accident	
06 Apr	Iraq (Basrah?)	AH-1W	USMC		nil	Iraqi fire	crew managed to land successfully
07 Apr	Tikrit	F-15E	USAF 333rd FS	88-1694 'SJ'	2 killed	Iraqi fire?	total loss
07 Apr	Baghdad	A-10A	USAF 75th FS	81-0987 FT	nil	Iraqi AAA	aircraft returned to base and repaired
07 Apr	Mediterranian Sea	SA-330J Puma	charter Geo-Seis Helicopters	N330JA '02'	nil	Iraqi fire	total loss

Date	Location	Type	Unit	Serial	Casualties	Cause	Level damage/ Result
08 Apr	Baghdad	A-10A	USANG 190th FS		pilot (172nd FS)rescued by CSAR	mechanical failure	total loss
08 Apr	Baghdad	A-10A	USANG 172th FS	80-0258 BC	nil	Iraqi SAM	repaired at base
08 Apr	Baghdad	A-10A	USANG 172th FS	80-0258	nil	accident	repaired at base
08 Apr	southern Iraq/ Saudi Arabia	HH-60H	US Navy HCS-5		nil		repaired
08 Apr	southern Iraq/ Saudi Arabia	UH-60A	US Navy HCS-5		nil		repaired
14 Apr	Samara	AH-1W	USMC MAG-39	163940	2 injured	accident	
30 Apr	Najaf	CH-53E	USMC HMH-465		nil		
02 May?	south Baghdad airport	Chinook HC2	RAF 27 Squadron		nil	accident after ran out of fuel	badly damaged
09 May	Samara	UH-60A	US Army 571st Med Coy	86-24507	3 killed, 1 injured	accident, flew into power cables	
19 May	Hillah	CH-46E	USMC HMM-364		4 crew and 1 rescuer killed	accident	total loss
27 May	Fallujah	UH-60A	US Army 3rd Infantry Division?				badly damaged
12 Jun	north-western Iraq	AH-64D	US Army 101st Division		nil	Iraqi fire	badly damaged
12 Jun	south-western Iraq	F-16CG USAF			nil	mechanical problem	total loss
24 Jun	Majar-al-Kabir	Chinook HC2	RAF 27 Squadron		7 injured	Iraqi fire	

Conclusion

Operation Iraqi Freedom saw extensive use of air power as part of a joint air, land and sea campaign to overthrow the government of Iraq. In the space of just under a month, US-led forces easily achieved their tactical and operational level objectives.

Air power was instrumental in almost every aspect of this campaign, from strategic reconnaissance, strike missions in Baghdad, air support for ground forces and air transport of vital supplies and personnel.

Apart from the gunners and missile crews of the Iraqi Air Defence Command, US, British and Australian airmen faced no organized resistance. Iraq's air force stayed on the ground for reasons that as yet are unclear. The number of aircraft shot down by hostile fire can be counted on one hand, and more US and British airmen died as a result of 'friendly fire' or in accidents than through enemy fire.

Much is still emerging as to how the campaign unfolded and why it ended as it did. Some issues are likely to gain prominence:

• Efforts to kill senior members of the Iraqi government, including Saddam Hussein himself, all ended in failure because of poor intelligence or delays in getting the information to strike aircraft.

• The majority of the US and British air effort was concentrated on destroying the Iraqi Republican Guard Forces Command south of Baghdad. This force appeared to be stationary and wide open to attack from the air.

• Heavy sand storms made many laser and optically guided weapons ineffective. This forced the US and British to rely heavily on satellite-guided weapons.

• Basing issues and overflight rights was a major complicating factor in US and British planning. Lavish air-to-air refuelling overcame many of these problems, but highlighted the need for tanker aircraft and long-range bombers.

• The lack of resistance makes it difficult to learn lessons about future air campaigns.

• On best estimates, some 5,000 to 7,000 Iraqi military personnel and civilians died and 20,000 were wounded during the war. Given the number of munitions employed, some 28,000, this was a relatively low number, but it demonstrates that there is no such thing as a 'casualty-free' war.

As this book was being completed, US and British troops were finding themselves increasingly under attack from Iraqi fighters opposed to the occupation of their country. While air power proved decisively effective during the campaign to overthrow the Iraqi government in Baghdad, it has had to take a supporting role in the occupation effort.

The final outcome of the US-led campaign to overthrow Saddam Hussein is still unclear, and future historians will judge if the effort was worthwhile.

Glossary

AAC	Army Air Corps (British Army)
AB	Air Base
AC	Air Component Co-ordination Element (USAF)
ACW	Air Control Wing (USAF)
AEG	Air Expeditionary Group (USAF)
AEW	Air Expeditionary Wing (USAF)
AG	Air Group (USAF)
AM	Air Marshal
AMW	Air Mobility Wing (USAF)
ARG	Air Refuelling Group (USAF)
ARS	Air Refuelling Squadron (USAF)
ARW	Air Refuelling Wing (USAF)
AS	Airlift Squadron (USAF)
AVM	Air Vice Marshal
Avn	Aviation (US Army)
AW	Airlift Wing (USAF)
AWACS	Airborne Warning and Control System
Bn	Battalion
Brig Gen	Brigadier General
BS	Bombardment Squadron (USAF)
BW	Bombardment Wing (USAF)
CAOC	Combined Air Operations Centre (USAF)
CFACC	Coalition Forces Air Component Commanders
CFLCC	Coalition Forces Land Component Commanders
Col	Colonel
CRG	Contingency Response Group (USAF)
CSAR	Combat search and rescue
Det	Detachment
ECS	Electronic Combat Squadron (USAF)
ELINT	Electronic Intelligence
ERS	Expeditionary Reconnaissance Squadron (USAF)
FAC	Forward Air Controller
FARP	Forward Arming and Refuelling Point
FG	Fighter Group (USAF)
Flt	Flight
FS	Fighter Squadron (USAF)
FW	Fighter Wing (USAF)
GBU	Guided Bomb Unit
Gen	General
Gp Capt	Group Captain
HARM	High-Speed Anti-Radiation Missile
HC	US Navy Helicopter Support Squadron
HCS	US Navy Helicopter Combat Support Squadron
HMH	US Marine Helicopter Squadron, Heavy
HMLA	US Marine Helicopter Attack Squadron, Light
HMM	US Marine Helicopter Squadron, Medium
HS	US Navy Helicopter Anti-submarine Squadron
HVM	High-Velocity Missile (UK SAM)
IAAF	Iraqi Army Air Corps
IADS	Integrated Air Defence System
IAEA	International Atomic Energy Agency
IQAF	Iraqi Air Force
Lt Col	Lieutenant Colonel
Lt Gen	Lieutenant General
LTW	Lynham Transport Wing (RAF)
Maj Gen	Major General
MAW	Marine Air Wing (USMC)
MEB	Marine Expeditionary Brigade (MEB)
MEF	Marine Expeditionary Force (USMC)
MEU	Marine Expeditionary Unit (USMC)
NAEWF	NATO Airborne Early-Warning Force
NAS	Naval Air Squadron (UK)
NATO	North Atlantic Treaty Organisation
NSA	National Security Agency (US)
RA	Royal Artillery
RAAF	Royal Australian Air Force
RAF	Royal Air Force (UK)
Regt	Regiment
RQS	Rescue Squadron (USAF)
RQW	Rescue Wing (USAF)
RS	Reconnaissance Squadron (USAF)
RW	Reconnaissance Wing (USAF)
SAM	Surface-to-Air Missile
SAS	Special Air Service (UK and Australia)
SEAD	Suppression of Enemy Air Defences
SLAM	Stand-off Land Attack Missile
SOAR	Special Operation Aviation Regiment (US Army)
SOG	Special Operations Group (USAF)
SOS	Special Operations Squadron (USAF)
SOW	Special Operations Wing (USAF)
Sqn	Squadron
TACP	Tactical Air Control Party
TDY	Temporary Duty (US military)
TF	Task Force
TLAM	Tomahawk Land Attack Missile
UN	United Nations
UNMOVIC	UN's Monitoring, Verification and Inspection Commission
UNSCOM	UN Special Commission
USAF	United States Air Force
USMC	US Marine Corps
USN	US Navy
USS	US Ship
VA	US Navy Attack Squadron
VAQ	US Navy Tactical Electronic Warfare Squadron
VAW	US Navy Carrier Airborne Early Warning Squadron
VF	US Navy Fighter Squadron
VFA	US Navy Strike Fighter Squadron
VMA	US Marine Attack Squadron
VMAQ	US Marine Tactical Electronic Warfare Squadron
VFMA	US Marine Fighter Attack Squadron
VFMA(AW)	US Marine All-Weather Fighter Attack Squadron
VMGR	US Marine Refuelling Squadron
VMU	US Marine Unmanned Aerial Vehicle unit
VP	US Navy Patrol Squadron
VQ	US Navy Fleet Reconnaissance Squadron
VS	US Navy Anti-submarine Squadron
Wg Cdr	Wing Commander

APPENDIX - AIR ORDER OF BATTLE
AIRCRAFT TYPE NUMBERS

USAF
Total 898
60 x A-10
8 x AC-130
11 x B-1
4 x B-2
28 B-52
5 x BQM-34
60 x F-16
71 x F-16CJ
42 x F-15
48 x F-15E
123 x F-117
10 x C-2

3 x C-20
7 x C-21
1 x C-32
1x C-40
5 x C-9
124 x C-130
7 x C-17
1 x CN-235
1 x DC-130
15 x E-3
7 x E-8
8 x EC-130
8 x HC-130
16 x HH-60

149 x KC-135
33 x KC-10
1 x NKC-135
7 x MQ-1
9 x RC-135
9 x RQ-1
1 x RQ-4
15 x U-2

USMC
Total 371
60 x F/A-18C/D
70 x AV-8B
58 x AH-1W
30 x UH-1

67 x CH-46
54 x CH-53
22 x KC-130T
10 x EA-6B

US Navy
Total 350
56 x F-14
176 x F/A-18C/E
25 x EA-6B
40 x S-3B
20 x E-2C
3 x EP-3
26 x P-3
4 x SH-3

US Army
Total 732
12 x RC-12
120 x AH-64D
60 x AH-64A
250 x UH-60
120 x OH-58D
170? x CH-47D/UH-1

US Special Operations Forces
Total 97
26 x MC-130

14 x MH-47
31 x MH-53
7 x MH-6
18 x MH-60
1 x PC-6

Australian
Total 22
3 x CH-47D
14 x F/A-18
3 x C-130H/J 2 x P-3

AIRCRAFT BASES & US UNITS

IRAQ (All opened up after US-led troops entered on 21st March)

Tallil Airbase- 392 AEW /A-10/AV-8B FARP/ 8 x HH-60 (301 RQS)

Bashur Airfield
86th CRG
6 x MH-53M (21 SOS)

Jallibah Airbase
USMC forward operating base/FARP

Al Kut Airbase (Blair Field)
USMC forward operating base/FARP

An Numaniyah Airbase
USMC forward operating base/FARP

Hantush Airfield
USMC forward operating base/FARP

Najaf
US Army forward operating base/FARP

Baghdad International Airport
US Army forward operating base/FARP

Umm Qasr Docks
UK forward operating base/FARP

Safwan
UK forward operating base/FARP

H-2 Airbase
US-UK Aus Special Forces forward operating base/FARP

H-1 Airbase
US-UK Aus Special Forces forward operating base/FARP

KUWAIT

Ali Al Salim Airbase- 386 AEW
RQ/MQ-1Predator UAV (15 ERS)
P-3 (VP-1, 40, 46, 47)
5 x RC-12 (US Arny V Corps)

HH-60 (38 RQS)
KC-130 (USMC)
HC-130 (939 RQW, 303 RQS?)
8 x MH-53M (20 SOS)
MC-130 (8 SOS)

Camp Coyote - I MEF/3 MAW
KC-130 (VMGR-234)
RQ-2 (VMU-2)

Ahmed Al Jaber Airbase- 322 AEW
18 x F-16CG (524 FS)
48 x A-10 (75, 303, 190, 172 FS)
36 x F/A-18C (VFMA-121, 232, 251)
24 x F/A-18D (VFMA-AW 225, 533)
24 x AV-8B (VMA 214, 542)
4 x HC-130/C-130E (39 RQS)
1 x UC-12 (3 MAW)

Camp Udairi/Iraq- 484 AEW
444 & 447 AEG (3,4, 18 Air Support Sqns) FAC Teams with US Army units

Kuwait International Airport
UK-US air transport hub

SAUDI ARABIA

Prince Sultan Air Base- 363 AEW
Combined Air Operations Center(CAOC)
200 US and UK aircraft
F-15C (67 FS)
F-16CJ (77FS, 35 FW)
5 x EA-6B (VMAQ-1)
E-3C AWACS (552 & 513 ACW)
E-8 JSTARS (116 ACW)
RC-135
KC-135 (92 ARW, 70 ARS)
2 x U-2 (99 RS)

Ar'ar Airport

US SF helicopter base
HH-60H (HCS 5)

Tabuk Airbase - 384 AEW??
KC-135 (916 ARS)

QATAR

Doha International Airport - 64 AEW
14 x C130 (317 AMW)
3 x C-130H/J (RAAF 36 Sqn)
EC-130H (41 ECS)
EC-130E? (193 SOW?)

Al Udeid Airbase - 379 AEW
12 x F-117 (8 FS)
48 x F-15E (333/334/336 FS)
F-16CJ (22/23 FS)
F-16C (157FS)
KC-10
KC-135 (911 ARS, 434 ARW)
1 x C40 (1 AS)
14 x F/A-18C (RAAF 75 Sqn)
2 x P-3 (92 Wing, RAAF)

OMAN

Thumrait Airbase - 405 AEW
11 x B-1 (34/37 BS)
KC-135 (92nd ARW, 931 ARG)
E-3 AWACS (552 & 513 ACW)

Masirah Airbase - 321st AEW/355 AEG
KC-135 (465 ARS, 336 ARS)
C-130 (167 AS)
Logistic support for Afghanistan

Seeb Airbase - 320 AEW/AEG
C130 (50, 39/40, 109, 189 AS)

UNITED ARAB EMIRATES

Al Dhafra - 380 AEW
10 x U-2 (99 RS)

1 x RQ-4 Global Hawk UAV (12 RS)
8 x KC-10 (60/305 AMW?)

BAHRAIN
Muharraq Airport
3 x EP-3 (VQ-1)
4 x P-3 (VP-1)
6 x CH-53 (HC-4)
3 x C-130 (USN)
4 x SH-3 (HC-2)
6 x C-2A (VRC-30)
Shaikh Isa Airbase - 358 AEW?
F-15C (71 FS, 58 FS)
C-130 (105, 130, 139, 142,
 165, 180, 185 AS)
KC-130 (VMGR-452)

JORDAN
Azraq Airbase, 410 AEW
RQ/MQ-1 UAV (15 RS/46ERS)
12 x A-10 (118 FS?)
F-16 (120, 160 FS)
4 x HC-130 (71 RQS)
HH-60 (66 RQS)
8 x AC-130 (4 SOS?)
MC-130 (8 SOS?)
17 x MH-53M (20 SOS?)
3 x CH-47D (5th Avn Regt, Australian Army)

BRITISH INDIAN OCEAN TERRITORY
Diego Garcia - 40 AEW
4 x B-2 (393 BS)
11x B-52 (20 &40BS)
12 x KC-135 (462 AEG/28 ARS)

US EUROPEAN COMMAND
TURKEY
Incirlik Air Base
Combined Air Forces North
headquarters
39 ASEW
50 x US and UK jets
E-3 AWACS(552 & 513 ACW)
16+ x F-16C (55 FS, 113 EFS(ANG))
F-15C (94 FS)
5 x EA-6B (VMAQ-?)
RC-135 (55 RW)
KC-135 (92, 900 ARS)
Konya Airbase
5/6 x E-3 AWAC (NATO)
Batman Airbase
Forward Airbase
Diyarbikar Airbase
Forward Airbase
US SF helicopter base
Van Airbase
Forward Airbase

GREECE
NSA Souda Bay, Crete - 398 AEG

RC-135 (55 RW)
1 x NKC-135 (412 Test Wing)
KC-135
3 x EC-130H (43 ECS)
1 x EP-3 (VQ-2)

CYPRUS
RAF Akrotiri - 401 AEW
29 x KC-135 (319th ARW, 163 ARW/
905,
351 153 ARS)
U-2 (99 RS)
4 x C-2 A(VRC-40)
2 x E-8 JSTARS (116 ACW/970
EAACS)
3 x E-3 AWACS(552 & 513 ACW)
5 x MH-53M (21 SOS)
2 x KC-130 (352 SOG)
1 x U-2

UNITED KINGDOM
RAF Fairford- 457 AEG
17 x B-52 (23 & 93 BS)
RAF Mildenhall - 171 AEW
18 x KC-135 KC-135E (171, 134, 190
ARW)
2 x HH-60G (58 RQS)
40 x C-141 (491 AEG/89, 356, 729,
730, 756 AS)

BULGARIA
Bourgas - 409 AEG
KC-10A (305&514 AMW, 507 ARW)

ROMANIA
Constanta-458th AEG
C-130E (37 AS)
HC-130 (??)
MC-130 (??)
6 x MH-53M (21 SOS) (moved to
Bashur/Akroiri)

GERMANY
Rhein Main Air Base- 362 AEG
C-17 (8, 14, 17 AS)

US NAVY CARRIER BATTLEGROUPS
Eastern Mediterranean
USS Theodore Roosevelt
V—-F-213 Blacklions, 10 x F-14D
VFA-15 Valions, 12 x F/A-18C
VFA-87 War Party, 12 x F/A-18C
VFA-201 Hunter,   12 x F/A-18C
VAQ-141 Shadowhawks, 4 x EA-6B
VS-24 Scouts, 8 x S-3B
VAW-124 Bear Aces, 4 x E-2C
USS Harry S Truman
VF-32, Swordsmen, 10 x F-14B
VFA-37 Bulls, 12 x F/A-18C
VFA-105 Gunslingers , 12 x F/A-18C
VMFA-115 Silver Eagles, 12 x F/A-18C
VAQ-130 Zappers, 4 x EA-6B

VS-22 Checkmates, 8 x S-3B
VAW-126 Seahaweks, 4 x E-2C
HS-7 Dusty Dogs, 4 x SH-60F, 2 x
HH-60H

ARABIAN GULF
USS Nimitz
(arrived early April)
VF-14, Tophatters, 12 x F/A-18E
VFA-41 Black Aces, 12 x F/A-18F
VFA-94 Mighty Shrikes, 12 x F/A-18C
VFA-97 Warhawks,   12 x F/A-18C
VAQ-135 Black ravens, 4 x EA-6B
VS-29 Dragonflies, 8 x S-3B
VAW-117 Wallbangers, 4 x E-2C
HS-6 Indians, 4 x SH-60F, 2 x HH-
60H
USS Abraham Lincoln
VF-31, Tomcatters, 10 x F-14D
VFA-25 First of the Fleet, 12 x F/A-18C
VFA-113 Stingers , 12 x F/A-18C
VFA-115 Eagles,   12 x F/A-18E
VAQ-139 Cougars, 4 x EA-6B
VS-35 Bluer Wolves, 8 x S-3B
VAW-113 Black Eagles, 4 x E-2C
HS-4 Black Knights, 4 x SH-60F, 2 x
HH-60H
USS Kitty Hawk
VF-154 Black Knights, 10 x F-14A
VFA-195 Dambusters, 12 x F/A-18C
VFA-192 Golden Dragons, 12 x F/A-
18C
VFA-27 Royal Maces, 12 x F/A-18C
VAQ-136 Gauntlets, 4 x EA-6B
VS-21 Fighting Red Tails, 8 x S-3B
VAW-115 Liberty Bells, 4 x E-2C
HS-14 Chargers, 4 x SH-60F, 2 x HH-
60H
USS Constellation
VF-12 Bounty Hunters, 10 x F-14B
VFA-137 Kestrels, 12 x F/A-18C
VFA-151 Vigilantes, 12 x F/A-18C
VMFA-323 Death Riders,   12 x F/A-
18C
VAQ-131 Lancers, 4 x EA-6B
VS-38 Red Griffinss, 8 x S-3B
VAW-116 Sun Kings, 4 x E-2C
HS-2 Golden Falcons, 4 x SH-60F, 2
x HH-60H

US MARINE CORPS HELICOPTER AND AV-8B UNITS
3rd Marine Air Wing
*Marine Air Groups 29 (CH-46/53) and
39 (AH-1/UH-1/CH-46)*
(forward deployed in Iraq)
HMLA-269, 369 (AH-1W, UH-1N)
HMM-165, 263 (CH-46E)
(Ali Al Salem, Kuwait)
HMM-162, 268, 364, 365 (CH-46E)

HMH-462, 464 (CH-53E)

AMPHIBIOUS WARFARE SHIPS ARABIAN GULF

AV-8B (elements VMA 211, 223, 231 and 311)

MH-53E (HM-14 & 15)(for mine sweeping)

USS *Bataan* (AV-8B)

USS *Bonhommie Richard* (AV-8B VMA-211)

USS *Kearsage* HMH-464 (CH-53E)

USS *Saipan* HM-14, 15 (MH-53E)

USS *Nassau* - 24th MEU (HMM-263, 12 CH-46E, 4 CH-53E, 3 UH-1N, 4 AH-1W, 6 AV-8B)

USS *Tarawa* - 15th MEU(HMM-161, 12 CH-46E, 4 CH-53E, 3 UH-1N, 4 AH-1W, 6 AV-8B)

MEDITERRANEAN SEA

(disembarked in mid April by air to Kurdistan)

USS *Iwo Jima* - 26th MEU (HMM-264, 12 CH-46E, 4 CH-53E, 3 UH-1N, 4 AH-1W, 6 AV-8B)

US ARMY HELICOPTER

V Corps

571st Medical Company (UH-60)

11th Aviation Brigade

2nd/6th Cavalry (21 x AH-64D, 6 x UH-60)

6th Squadron, 6th Cavalry Regiment (21 x AH-64A, 6 x UH-60)

1st Battalion, 227th Aviation Regiment (attached from 1st Cav Div) (21 x AH-64D, 6 x UH-60)

12th Aviation Brigade

F Company, 159th Aviation (15 x CH-47D)

5th Battalion, 158th Aviation Regiment (UH-60 and CH-47)

3rd Battalion, 158th Aviation Regiment (UH-60 and CH-47)

D Compay 1-159th Aviation Regiment

2nd Brigade, 82nd Airborne Division

1st Battalion, 82nd Aviation Regiment (OH-58D)\

3rd Infantry Division (Mechanised)

4th Aviation Brigade

1st Battalion, 3rd Aviation Regiment (21 x AH-64D, 6 x UH-60) ,

2st Battalion, 3rd Aviation Regiment (40 x UH-60, 4 x EH-60,

3/7 Cav (16 x OH-58D, 4 x UH-60)

101st Airborne (Air Assault) Division (270 helicopters)

101st Aviation Brigade

2-17 Cav (32x OH-58D)

1st Battalion, 101st Aviation Regiment (21 x AH-64D, 6 x UH-60)

2nd Battalion, 101st Aviation Regiment (21 x AH-64D, 6 x UH-60)

3rd Battalion, 101st Aviation Regiment (21 x AH-64A, 6 x UH-60)

6th Battalion, 101st Aviation Regiment (24 x UH-60)

159th Aviation Brigade

4th Battalion, 101st Aviation Regiment (24 x UH-60)

5th Battalion, 101st Aviation Regiment (30 x UH-60)

7th Battalion, 101st Aviation Regiment (48 x CH-47)

9th Battalion, 101st Aviation Regiment (30 x UH-60)

4th Infantry Division (Mechanised)

4th Aviation Brigade

1st Battalion, 4th Aviation Regiment (21 x AH-64D, 6 x UH-60)

2st Battalion, 4th Aviation Regiment (40 x UH-60, 4 x EH-60

1/10th Cav (8 x OH-58D)

BRITISH AIR DEPLOYMENTS
Total 227 aircraft and helicopters
(all squadrons/units RAF except where marked)

Incirlik, Turkey: 4 Jaguar GR3, 1 VC10 (10/101 Sqn)

Akrotiri, Cyprus: 1 VC10 medivac, 8 C130K/J (LTW)

Iraq, Jordan/Western Iraq: 8 Harrier GR7 (3 Sqn), 2 Canberra PR9 (39 Sqn), 8 Chinook (7 Sqn), 6 x Lynx AH7 (657 Sqn AAC)

Kuwait, Ali al Salem: 18 Tornado GR4 (II Sqn, 9 Sqn, 31 Sqn, 617 Sqn)

Kuwait, Ahmed al Jaber: 12 Harrier GR7 (IV Sqn)

Kuwait/Iraq (1 UK Armd Div); 4 Pheonix UAV launcher and 29 air vehicles (32 Regt RA)

Saudi Arabiam Prince Sultan AB: 14 Tornado F3 (43, 111 Sqns) 2 HS125 (32 Sqn), 4 E3D AWACS (8/23 Sqn), 4 Nimrod MR2 120/201/206 Sqn), 7 VC10 (10/101 Sqn), 1 Nimrod R1 (51 Sqn)

Bahrain, Muharraq: 4 Tristar (216 sqn)

Qatar, Al Udeid: 12 Tornado GR4 (II Sqn, 12 Sqn, 617 Sqn) 1 HS125 (32 Sqn)

UAE: 4 C130K/J (LTW)

Oman, Seeb: 2 Nimrod MR2 (120/201/206 Sqn)

Kuwait, Ali al Salem and Iraq FOB (Joint Helicopter Force): 6 Chinook (18 Sqn), 7 Puma (33 Sqn), 12 Lynx and 10 Gazelles (3 Regt AAC - Attached 16 Air Assault Brigade)

HMS *Ocean* (Commando Helicopter Force): 10 Sea King (845 NAS), 6 Lynx and 6 Gazelle (847 NAS)

HMS *Ark Royal*: 5 Chinook (18 Sqn - Joint Helicopter Force), 4 Sea King AEW7 (849 NAS)

RFA *Fort Victoria*: 4 Merlin of 814 (NAS)

RFA *Argus*, RFA *Austin* and RFA *Rosalie*: 6 Sea King Mk6 (820 NAS) in hack role.

HMS *Liverpool*, HMS *Edinburgh*, HMS *York*, MS *Marlborough*

HMS *Richmond*, HMS *Chatham* (2 x Lynx), HMS *Cardiff*: Total 9 Lynx HAS3/HMA8 (815 NAS)